CONSTELLATIONS

Like the future itself, the imaginative possibilities of science fiction are limitless. And the very development of cinema is inextricably linked to the genre, which, from the earliest depictions of space travel and the robots of silent cinema to the immersive 3D wonders of contemporary blockbusters, has continually pushed at the boundaries. **Constellations** provides a unique opportunity for writers to share their passion for science fiction cinema in a book-length format, each title devoted to a significant film from the genre. Writers place their chosen film in a variety of contexts – generic, institutional, social, historical – enabling **Constellations** to map the terrain of science fiction cinema from the past to the present... and the future.

'This stunning, sharp series of books fills a real need for authoritative, compact studies of key science fiction films. Written in a direct and accessible style by some of the top critics in the field, brilliantly designed, lavishly illustrated and set in a very modern typeface that really shows off the text to best advantage, the volumes in the **Constellations** series promise to set the standard for SF film studies in the 21st century.'
Wheeler Winston Dixon, Ryan Professor of Film Studies, University of Nebraska

 Constellations

 Constelbooks

Also available in this series

12 Monkeys Susanne Kord

Blade Runner Sean Redmond

Brainstorm Joseph Maddrey

Children of Men Dan Dinello

Close Encounters of the Third Kind Jon Towlson

The Damned Nick Riddle

Dune Christian McCrea

Ex Machina Joshua Grimm

Inception David Carter

Jurassic Park Paul Bullock

Mad Max Martyn Conterio

RoboCop Omar Ahmed

Rollerball Andrew Nette

Stalker Jon Hoel

Forthcoming

Mr. Freedom Tyler Sage

The OA David Sweeney

Seconds Jez Conolly & Emma Westwood

The Stepford Wives Samantha Lindop

CONSTELLATIONS

Lost

Brigid Cherry

Dedication

For Isla, may you never be lost.

Acknowledgements

Writing this book, and rewatching *Lost*, has been an enjoyable and productive experience, but it could not have taken place without the help and support of many people. I would particularly like to acknowledge the support of my colleagues at St Mary's University during the development of this project. The students who took my course on cult film and television also deserve a mention and I would like to thank them for their contributions to various seminar discussions. I would also like to thank John Atkinson, the editor of the Constellations series at Auteur/Liverpool University Press, for taking on this project. Finally, and most importantly, I would like to acknowledge Brian Robb, who originally came up with the idea for this book and encouraged me to pursue the project. His inspiration and thought-provoking discussion are always appreciated.

First published in 2021 by
Auteur, an imprint of Liverpool University Press,
4 Cambridge Street, Liverpool L69 7ZU
www.liverpooluniversitypress.co.uk/imprints/Auteur/
Copyright © Auteur 2021

Series design: Nikki Hamlett at Cassels Design
Set by Cassels Design www.casselsdesign.co.uk

All rights reserved. No part of this publication may be reproduced in any material form (including photocopying or storing in any medium by electronic means and whether or not transiently or incidentally to some other use of this publication) without the permission of the copyright owner.

British Library Cataloguing-in-Publication Data
A catalogue record for this book is available from the British Library

ISBN paperback: 978-1-80085-923-4
ISBN hardback: 978-1-80085-922-7
ISBN epub: 978-1-80085-806-0
ISBN PDF: 978-1-80034-395-5

Contents

Introduction: The Crash 7

Chapter 1: The Beach 19

Chapter 2: The Hatch 33

Chapter 3: The Barracks 45

Chapter 4: The Freighter 59

Chapter 5: The Orchid 71

Chapter 6: The Temple 83

Afterword: The Lamp Post 93

Notes 96

References 97

Introduction: The Crash

From its opening moments featuring the aftermath of a plane crash on a tropical island *Lost* (2004-10) became one of the most intriguing and talked about television programmes in the era of digital media. Yet what is it about this drama series that so captivates? In many respects, it is because *Lost* itself is a mystery. This is not to say that it is unknown or unknowable, but that as a cultural text the narrative is constructed around a series of mysteries and the plotlines deliberately raise more questions than they answer. That these narrative enigmas are presented as a genre hybrid of science fiction, adventure series, and reality TV only deepens the intrigue. Moreover, the story itself carries over into its paratexts – this extra-textual narrative material includes a novel, a videogame, short scenes available online, interactive online games, and even the merchandising such as jigsaw puzzles. To be drawn into the fictional world of *Lost* is to become a detective of sorts – a solver of mysteries and a collector of clues. The narration on the promotional trailer for *Lost: Missing Pieces*, for example, directs avid viewers into taking on this role. These missing pieces are a series of thirteen two- to three-minute long 'mobisodes' distributed prior to the fourth season in 2008 on the Verizon mobile network and the ABC website that fill in narrative gaps in the first three seasons of *Lost*.[1] The trailer offers the potential viewer: 'New scenes, new clues, a new chance to get into the mystery of *Lost*', while a character (Ben Linus, in a clip from the series) tantalizingly promises 'I have information you need'. As this indicates, viewers need clues and information in order to be able to understand the 'mystery of *Lost*'. Developed and extended over its six seasons, this mystery forms the core of the narrative. In telling the stories of the plane crash survivors on the island and beyond, nothing is ever quite what it seems and answers only generate more questions.

Getting There: The Making of *Lost*

Although *Lost* ultimately turned out to be a complex narrative construction imbued with science fiction tropes, at its outset the premise was much more straightforward. An idea for a series about the survivors of a plane crash was first suggested by ABC

Entertainment president Lloyd Braun on a management retreat in 2003 at a time when the network was desperate to generate fresh ideas since it had fallen behind NBC, CBS and Fox in the ratings (Sellers 2004). The inspiration was *Cast Away* (2000), the film about a systems engineer who must learn how to survive alone on a deserted island after a plane crash (Bernstein 2007). Quoted by David Bernstein (2007), Thom Sherman, then a senior vice-president of ABC, said that the idea was not taken seriously because it was reminiscent of *Gilligan's Island* (1964-67). Despite it being rejected at the meeting, Sherman discussed the idea with Ted Gold from Spelling Productions where an idea for a similar fictional drama series, this time based on the reality TV hit *Survivor* (2000-), was being considered. Sherman and Gold commissioned screenwriter Jeffrey Lieber, then on a blind deal contract to Spelling (an agreement for a future unspecified project), to develop a script for a pilot. The series was thus, from its outset, one that combined and hybridised different generic forms and ideas (notably realism and character-driven drama). Working from ABC's high concept – a hyper-realistic depiction of survivors on an uninhabited tropical island – Lieber pitched his outline for a series which was at that point titled *Nowhere*. Lieber saw it as a 'realistic show about a society putting itself back together after a catastrophe' (Bernstein 2007), envisaging it as a grown-up version of *The Lord of the Flies* (William Golding's 1954 novel about schoolboys trying to survive on an island after a plane crash). The plot at this point centred on a number of key characters including a doctor, a conman, a fugitive, a pregnant woman, a drug-addict, a military officer, and a spoiled rich girl. Even casual viewers of *Lost* can instantly recognise these characters in Jack, Sawyer, Kate, Claire, Charlie, Sayid and Shannon. Lieber's outline also featured half-brothers vying for the leadership role, and again these central antagonists and the underlying conflict can be identified in Jack and Locke. Just as with the generic hybridity, the themes of the series were present early in the development history, and these too were organised around multiple characters and conflicts. What is not present at this stage though are the mystery and the increasingly dominant science fiction elements. It was only with further development and the handing of the outline to writer and show runner J.J. Abrams – already established as a cult auteur with a fan following from his work on *Alias* (2001-6) – that the core elements of *Lost* emerged, and it was these that would lend the series its unique qualities.

Braun is quoted in *New York* magazine (Rosen 2010) as saying he was unhappy with Lieber's rewrites and was not prepared to put the resulting script into production. Although with the basic narrative elements in place Lieber's writing credit was assured by the Writer's Guild arbitration (Craig 2005), most of the core concepts of *Lost* were introduced when Abrams and co-writer Damon Lindelof were brought in. The production of a two-hour pilot was rushed ahead from Abrams and Lindelof's 22-page outline (Rosen 2010). The fact that the series was green-lit without a script was itself an extremely unusual production decision, further marking out *Lost* as a significant moment in television history. Quoted in *Chicago* magazine, Sherman acknowledges that: 'I don't know if there's another [production] like this in the annals of television' (Bernstein 2007). As with other keynote series, it is creative vision that is a defining characteristic, and in this case Abrams and Lindelof were supported by Braun, who shared their vision. Braun, quoted in the *Los Angeles Times*, said of the Abrams outline: 'It's the best piece of television I've ever read. I was out of my mind. I knew it would make noise that would be so big, so different, you couldn't avoid it' (Fernandez 2005).

Within three months *Lost* was in production (Bernstein 2007) and the two-part pilot (shot as a two-hour episode, though transmitted in two parts) was completed in twelve weeks (Craig 2005). It is also worth noting that *Lost* was the most expensive pilot that had been made up to that point, costing between $11 and $12 million (Fernandez 2005). The production costs reflect the significant undertaking of the production, involving location shooting in Hawaii and the special effects required to create the plane crash and wreckage on the beach. These aspects of the production are significant in that they create a level of televisuality, spectacle and authenticity in the action and setting that would be unlikely in a studio-bound production. The series also had the largest ensemble cast of American television drama up to that time. With fourteen actors being given star billing, this was larger than that for other ensemble series of the time including *The West Wing* (1999-2006) with nine, *ER* (1994-2009) with seven for its first season, and *Alias* with eight. In fact, the large cast permitted the organisation of the narrative around multiple character story arcs intersecting with 'a sci-fi premise' that 'created a compelling detailed universe' (Hilmes 2011: 426).

The impacts behind the scenes of such an expensive and elaborate production have already been noted in James B. Stewart's *DisneyWar* (2006). Disney-ABC, which owned ABC Entertainment, was concerned about the costs. Disney CEO Michael Eisner has been reported as calling *Lost* 'another crazy Abrams project' and COO Robert Iger as thinking it would never work as a series (Craig 2005). The Disney executives were concerned about both the cost of the pilot and the fact that Abrams and Lindelof had no clear idea of what the mysterious monster on the island was. As Stewart speculates: 'If Eisner or Iger decided they wanted rid of [Braun], he'd handed them the ammunition: he had green-lit a $12 million pilot that still didn't have a script' (2006: 487). However, it is rare in Hollywood for a production to be shut down once shooting has begun and money has been committed. Braun was correct in saying that: 'If we are pregnant enough, they won't shut us down' (quoted in Craig 2005), though he became a scapegoat for the risk-averse Hollywood television industry and was fired. Despite the misgivings, *Lost* became not only a ratings success, but also a popular culture phenomenon. The key element in this was the introduction of elements that appeared at first paranormal and were later revealed as science fictional into the narrative. It was these – provided by Abrams and Lindelof – that so excited Braun.

Getting *Lost*: The Making of a Cult Science Fiction Series

Aspects of the production background as outlined above can be seen as symptomatic of the battle between commerce and artistry, an example of the allocative struggle that epitomises Hollywood (see also Porter and Lavery 2006: 18). Like many texts that are also regarded as significant examples of quality must-see television on the one hand and cult TV on the other – a 'cult blockbuster' as Stacey Abbott (2009) terms it – *Lost* is the singular vision of the creative team, a key factor in the appeal for fan audiences. Whilst on the one hand this may raise concerns (especially for network executives) that the scriptwriter or showrunner do not know how the storylines will develop or how the series will conclude, on the other this can open up possibilities for the kind of narrative creativity that produces fresh or innovative programming and attracts avid fan interest. Significantly, the absence of a script may not always mean that the creative team are making it up as they go along. In his account of *Lost* as 'mastermind narration', Morris Clarke (2010: 124) observes that the 'perceived precariousness of writing television programmes' is now commonplace with respect to series that experiment with the techniques of storytelling. As Abrams has stated: 'the lack of development was one of the greatest assets for *Lost* – we didn't have time to second-guess what we were doing and sanitise it into a more middle-ground story' (Horkins 2005). The spontaneity and freedom to innovate that this implies can thus be linked to the resulting production having the hallmarks of quality television, with imagination and innovation not being compromised by pragmatic or financial concerns.

Although debates about what constitutes 'quality television' are still ongoing, as set out by Kristin Thompson (2003) key traits include narrative complexity with multiple plot threads and arc stories continuing across many episodes, open-ended or unresolved plotlines and narrative ambiguity, large ensemble casts and a high degree of psychological realism. Given these characteristics, it seems likely that even major storylines will be under-developed in the planning stages, as *Lost*'s were, and furthermore this builds flexibility and potential for dramatic twists and new developments into the series. Eisner and Iger's concerns that the series had gone into production without a completed script also seem misplaced when the defining factor of *Lost* is mystery, as Abrams, Lindelof and others have all stated frequently in interviews. Far from narrative precariousness, this represents an opening up of potential for creative narrative developments. Certainly, this is often the case with series seen as being under the creative control of a cult auteur or showrunner, and the evidence as drawn from interviews with Abrams, Lindelof and Carlton Cuse (who stepped in to Abrams' position during season one when Abrams left to work on film projects) suggests this is true of *Lost*. As Henry Jenkins points out, extra-textual discourses allow a series' creator to 'articulate a personal vision' (1995: 189). Talking about the development of the pilot episode, Abrams and Lindelof both set out their intentions for the underlying mystery of *Lost*. Lindelof has stated in *The Genesis of Lost* documentary[2] that his ideas were: 'all about mystery. A mystery of who the people were that were in the crash, and a mystery of what the island was that they crashed on.' In the same documentary, Abrams' comments similarly foreground the notion of mystery: 'What if the island wasn't just an island. And what if they found a hatch on the island. And this weird little thing for me was a nugget [...] that could be kind of cool.' Furthermore, Lindelof's idea for episodes organised around flashbacks provided structure to the narrative, offering both a regular format and wide variety of settings, moods and tones. Crucially, Abrams employed Jesse Alexander and Jeff Pinker on *Lost*, both of whom had worked with him on *Alias* and therefore clearly understood his vision. In particular, this meant that the writers, executive consultants and co-executive producers on the series were part of a cohesive team that could, as Alexander states in the documentary, work to develop the 'compelling mystery in a way that we had touched on in *Alias*, with building a mythology and a serialised mystery'.

It is an interest in the enigmatic in particular that has been articulated in the context of *Lost*. In a 2007 TED talk,[3] Abrams spoke about *Lost* in relation to a 'mystery box' his grandfather had bought him in a magic shop when he was a child: 'The thing is, it represents infinite possibility. It represents hope. It represents potential. [...] Mystery is the catalyst for imagination. [...] There are times where mystery is more important than knowledge.' The concept of the island as a place of unexplained events and paranormal phenomena, maintaining a set of enigma codes throughout its six seasons, makes *Lost* Abrams' (and by extension Lindelof and Cuse's) mystery box. In this way, *Lost* is an important example of telefantasy (Johnson 2005, 2-3). Telefantasy is not a clearly defined generic category; rather it is a mix of fantasy, horror, science fiction and even cop shows and spy dramas with fantastical elements. In fact, *Lost* can be considered alongside *Life on Mars* (2006-7) in terms of its hero's temporal dislocation and *The Prisoner* (1967-68) with its protagonist trapped in an isolated location with unstable geographical coordinates, as much as it does the convoluted timelines of *Doctor Who* (1963-) under showrunner Steven Moffat and the conspiracy-induced paranoia of *The X-Files* (1993-2002; 2016-18). Although it is not straightforwardly classifiable as science fiction, *Lost*'s generic hybridity as a key telefantasy series with strong science fiction themes means it is worthy of consideration as a landmark television series.

Getting It: *Lost* and its Audience

When *Lost* crash-landed on the television landscape on 22 September 2004, it came fifteenth in that week's Nielsen ratings. Whilst the audience figures were substantially lower than the top-ranking drama *CSI* (2000-15), it nonetheless compared favorably with the first season of *CSI* which averaged 17.8 million and was ranked tenth. *Variety* reported that it 'opened to surprisingly socko numbers for the Alphabet, dominating its timeslot with the best young-adult rating for a drama premiere on any net (excluding spinoffs) in four years' (Kissell 2004: 1). Kissel goes on to report that:

> *Lost* (6.8/20 in adults 18-49, 18.65 million viewers overall) took the 8 o'clock hour in every ratings category from kids to 50-plus. It showed broad appeal in key young-adult demos and among both genders. [...] No drama premiere on any net (excluding *CSI* spinoffs) has opened to a higher 18-49 rating since NBC's *Ed* in October 2000.

This audience was, at least in no small part, attracted by the extensive publicity in the run up to the launch of the series. Quoted by Kissell (2004), ABC Entertainment president Steve McPherson credits this to the 'exhaustive marketing campaign' which included radio and billboard ads as well as the TV trailers. The 25-second teaser[4] depends on fast cutting between shots of the key characters, the plane crash and the wreckage on the beach. It first sells the series by linking it to cult auteur Abrams: 'From J.J. Abrams' and 'The creator of *Alias*' is doubly emphasised via on-screen splash text that fills the screen (the lettering is cut out from shots of the fireball from the crashed plane) and authoritative voice-over (the narration is in deep, masculine tones). More importantly perhaps, this trailer immediately sells the series by setting up key points of intrigue, again in splash text and voice-over: '48 survivors', '1000 miles off course' and 'They survived the worst' overlaid with dialogue clips of the pilot's 'What the hell was that?' and Claire's 'Did anyone see that?'. It then questions the characters' survival with splash text and voice-over asking 'Or did they?'. Clips of Sawyer shooting at a polar bear (which in the trailer just appears as a large white creature running through the undergrowth towards the camera) and Kate screaming suggest that the answer here is no, they did not. It ends by compounding the mystery and danger with a close-up of Charlie asking (on behalf of the viewer perhaps), 'Guys, where are we?'. The series of questions drawing attention to the central mystery were also a feature of *Life on Mars*, which ran during seasons 2 and 3 of *Lost*, with its 'Is he mad? In a coma? Or back in time?' tagline. In his account of this series, Robin Nelson points out that a central mystery, with a suggestion of science fiction elements, contribute significantly to cult status (2010: 143).

The international marketing was similarly significant. In the UK, the trailers for the Channel 4 network were also notable for being directed by renowned photographer David LaChapelle. *Lost* launched in the UK on 10 August 2005, and although word might already have been expected to have spread given its acclaim in the US, Channel 4 spent an undisclosed, yet significant, sum of money on LaChapelle's trailer. According to *The Guardian* (Wilson 2005) it cost upwards of £1.5 million, with Polly Cochrane, C4's director of marketing, quoted as saying that rival network Sky spends £1-1.5 million promoting series and that Channel 4 therefore had to 'up their level' accordingly. The article goes on to offer Channel 4's defence of the expensive trailer as 'lavish, semi-cryptic campaigns are part of a conscious strategy', that '*Lost* [is an] extremely classy show and you want those production values to be echoed in the marketing', and that since 'the opening episode of *Lost* is, at over $5m, the most expensive pilot ever made[, s]pending big to give it a fair shout in an already crowded market is the least it deserves – you only launch once.' Cochrane also states that the trailer was designed 'to allow the personality and tone of the show to speak through the marketing', playing up its telefantasy status by saying it is 'a surreal concoction, so it merits a cryptic trailer'.

This trailer significantly enhanced the mystery by giving away nothing about the plot beyond the beach location with the plane wreckage and showing the principal cast members, dressed in torn and disheveled formal wear, dancing in slow motion. The version for E4 (generally referred to as the music version) used the Portishead track *Numb* and a second version screened on Channel 4 (the voice-over version) used dialogue spoken by cast members over Channel 1 Suite by The Cinematic Orchestra.[5] Both versions explored the mystery and intrigues surrounding the characters: Kate is shown dancing with both Jack and Sawyer, Sun moves between Jin and Michael, Locke is depicted as a conductor (figure 1). These images provide clues to events and character roles that will only be revealed slowly as the season progresses. In the music version, the Portishead lyrics clearly signal specific themes for the characters: I'm never so lost (Charlie); Been searching (Locke); A turning, a turning from deceit (Kate and Sawyer); I can't understand myself anymore (Sawyer turning to camera);

Figure 1: Locke conducts the dancing on the beach in David LaChapelle's trailer (© Channel 4)

'Cause I'm still feeling lonely (Sayid and Shannon); Feelin' so unholy (Kate with Jack); And this loneliness, It just won't leave me alone (Clair, no longer pregnant, sitting before the burning engine). The voice-over version layers multiple voices and repetitions of character descriptions into a tone poem:

> All of us have a secret. One of us is a hero. One of us is a fraud. One of us is a junkie. One of is a cop. One of us is a sinner. One of us is a saint. One of us is a martyr. One of us is a murderer. All of us are guilty. All of us are lost.

Again, this suggests character themes, prefigures the central mysteries and draws potential viewers into questioning the role of each character. These hooks were clearly enough to attract a similarly substantial audience to that in the US. In the UK, the first episode was watched by an audience of six million (BBC News 2005).

The US media reviews for the opening episode (1.1 'Pilot part 1') were extremely positive; as Kissell points out, it 'generated the best reviews for any programme this fall' (2004). The review in *Entertainment Weekly*, for example, mirrors the teaser's constructed response. The review focuses first on Abrams as a cult figure – 'he's developed a hardcore fan base that will follow [...] wherever his imagination takes him' (Tucker 2004). This positions Abrams as a producer of intelligent genre television who brings to *Lost* an established following of devoted viewers. Tucker then explores how the trailer pulls the viewer into its mysteries:

> Very quickly, you really want to know what's up with the large young hippieish fellow (Jorge Garcia) whose geniality radiates calm. By contrast, you want to know why Terry O'Quinn (a familiar baldy from *The X-Files* and *Alias*) distances himself from everyone and gives off a spooky vibe. This is the kind of show in which an apparent main character, Monaghan's rock star, has both a drug habit and the key, climactic line that speaks for everyone: 'Guys – where are we?'

The review concludes by confirming that the mystery is working: 'It's the kind of show where I have to write "apparent" a lot because I know there are going to be lots of unexpected revelations about the islanders' identities and motives.' There is every indication that the strategy – to get viewers drawn into the mystery with the trailers and the opening episode – worked, as Tucker adds in his review: 'I was yearning to see a second hour right away'.

Not all reviews of *Lost* during its first season were so positive. *The Guardian*, for example, suggests that it is 'a sprawling and unsatisfactory mess with no resolution in sight. It's not teasing the audience, it's senselessly fragmented. It's not resurrecting the art of deferred gratification, it has entirely lost its way. It is, in short, over' (Mangan 2005). Audiences did fall, from an average of 16 million across season one to 13 million for season four. Across the series, viewing figures ranged from a high of 23.47 million for the opening episode of season two to a low of 7.1 million for the final episode of season four. In comparison the final episode was watched by 13.5 million viewers in the US, though this was the highest figure achieved through seasons five and six (Ausiello 2010). Although this indicates a decline of live viewing, it does not necessarily imply waning interest in the series, as evidenced by high DVD box set sales (the season four set selling over one million units in the first five weeks of its release). Jonathan Gray also argues that viewing of the series via streaming and downloads, especially in overseas markets, mean the traditional audience measures are underestimates (2008: 79). Although the series did lose viewers and some of its critical acclaim over its six-year run, Mangan's assumptions that the viewer's attention was 'too thinly spread' and the story arcs caused a 'faint weariness' to creep over the audience seem overstated and not born out by either first-run audiences or the intensity of a core cult audience. *Lost* clearly established and maintained a high profile despite (in Mangan's words) 'the odds stacked against it'.

It may be that, at least to some extent, the increasingly complex narrative was off-putting to casual viewers (even with a recap clips-show at the start of later seasons). Beyond the mainstream audience ratings and the media coverage, however, the science fictional contexts of the series can be seen as the root of *Lost*'s cult appeal, and its significance as a programme ideally fitted to the era of digital media, cultural convergence and transmedia storytelling (Pearson 2007). It is an intensely involving and yet frustratingly complex series, one that invites endless speculation over its increasingly convoluted narrative. It blends mythology, mysticism, conspiracy theory and conflict in a way that makes for a highly polysemic text, offering something for everyone in its broad and ethnically diverse character range, its generic hybridity and its thematic diversity, and – consolidating its cult appeal for online fan cultures – it cannot be contained by the televisual narrative alone but spills over on to the Internet, mobile telephony and podcasts. Arriving with perfect timing to exploit the conjunction of online gaming, mobile Internet access and viral marketing technologies (such as the *Lost: Missing Pieces* discussed above), *Lost* became an interactive viewing experience that had to be tracked across different formats, carrying the core fan audience into the realm of mobisodes, webisodes and alternate reality games (ARGs). It was 'compulsive, addictive television' (Craig 2005), becoming both the must-see-TV and must-click-TV of the mid- to late-2000s, generating ritualistic viewing practices and devotion to the text.

In this way *Lost* invited its audience into a game of guesswork and strategy, and it worked to maintain cult appeal. Furthermore, *Lost* came to be regarded as an important example of quality television that continued the trend towards mainstream TV embracing science fiction and telefantasy. In listing it among the 'Ten Shows that changed TV since '90', *Entertainment Weekly* describes it as: 'The great gamble that paid off: a six-season puzzle on an epic scale, with scores of characters and intricate plotting that truly put the myth in "mythology". *Lost* altered our view of the size and shape and momentum a TV series could maintain' (Tucker 2010). The features of the series recognised here place *Lost* in a category of groundbreaking entertainment alongside other innovative telefantasy such as *Twin Peaks* (1990-91; 2017), *The X-Files*, and *Buffy the Vampire Slayer* (1997-2003) – all of which are on *Entertainment Weekly*'s list. *Lost* is a prime example of an unpredictable generic hybrid that roots its science fiction elements in a realistic scenario. It subverts expectations while being a satisfying and mind-blowing experience. Its fragmented narrative is a literal puzzle that transcends the constraints of television drama. It has proved that transmedia storytelling can carry an audience beyond the medium of television itself. It is no wonder that Eonline called *Lost* 'the most fascinating show on TV' (Team WWK 2008).

In the chapters that follow, the narrative codes, generic conventions and transmedia storytelling techniques of the series are analysed in order to position *Lost* in relation to science fiction, telefantasy and cult media. Chapter 1 sets out the traits of the cult text – the perpetuated hermeneutic and the hyperdiegesis – in terms of puzzles and maps. Chapter 2 looks at the neo-baroque aesthetic of *Lost*, particularly the narrative's organisation around games and game play. Chapter 3 explores the themes of community, gender and identity, considering in particular the discourses organised around femininity and reproductive technology. Chapter 4 analyses the themes of science and technology, looking at conspiracy and time travel as tropes of the science fiction genre. Chapter 5 extends the discussion of science fiction into the philosophical, exploring power and control in the surveillance society. Finally, chapter 6 considers *Lost*'s significance as a transmedia and hypertextual narrative.

Chapter 1: The Beach

As Marc Dolan points out, *Lost* is 'a peculiar hybrid: a mainstream cult show' (2010: 149). As outlined in the introduction, it has the wide appeal, high ratings and strong critical reception of a mainstream hit. Nevertheless, in turning to the narrative construction, the traits of the cult television series can be identified. Using science fiction tropes in the ongoing arc story means that *Lost* has a structuring narrative code in much the same way as *The X-Files* established a decade before. This works to maintain a narrative that never attains complete closure, which in combination with interweaving multiple character storylines across many timelines and dispersed locations, produces a rich storyworld. In many ways such traits are similar to those of the soap opera's open-ended narrative structure (Fiske 1987) or classic American quality television such as *Hill Street Blues* (1981-87), which Dolan describes as the 'setting-orientated, departing actor-proof tradition' (2010: 150). However, in terms of its complex diegesis and (lack of) resolution, the narrative of *Lost* is rather more mythic in scale and ultimately possesses far less realism than might be expected of the soap opera or mainstream drama series. In fact, these narrative traits, what Jason Mittell calls 'narrative complexity' (2015: 54), are a defining feature of cult telefantasy series such as *Twin Peaks* and *The OA* (2016-19), as well as *The X-Files*. Matt Hills (2004) defines the narrative attributes of cult television as the perpetuated hermeneutic and the hyperdiegesis. The perpetuated hermeneutic (Tulloch and Alvarado 1983: 133) is an open-ended narrative form that repeats familiar characteristics whilst endlessly deferring resolution (Hills 2004: 101). The set of questions around which the series is focused (in *Lost* these include Who are the Others?, What is inside the hatch?, What is the meaning of the numbers?, Charlie's 'Guys, where are we?') drives the deferred narrative and 'leaves space open for further speculation beyond the bounds of the original text' (Johnson 2005: 2). Similarly, the hyperdiegesis is an unfinished, albeit internally logical and stable, fictional world. Hills defines it as a 'vast and detailed narrative space, only a fraction of which is ever directly seen or encountered within the text' (2004: 104). The implied narrative world is thus much larger than that which is explicitly represented (in *Lost* this includes organisations and characters such as Mittellos Biosciences and Alvar Hanso, as well as places and past events such as the multiple references to Portland or the building of the three-toed statue). The series constructs a hyperdiegesis which, like the perpetuated hermeneutic, opens up the space for creative speculation (Hills 2004: 104). Each new season of *Lost* introduces new narrative elements and ambiguities, but a perpetuated hermeneutic and a hyperdiegesis can be identified from the very start.

Narrative as Enigma

As explored by the analysis of the promotional material in the introduction, enigma, suspense, tortuous cause and effect chains, and open-ended plotlines were the hallmarks of *Lost*. These are all established in the opening two-parter, 1.1/2 'Pilot', along with several science fictional elements that will become ongoing narrative arcs (though the viewer is not necessarily aware of these on first viewing). These include the smoke monster, Danielle's distress signal, and the displaced polar bears. Also established early in season one are the island's strange properties, including miraculous healing. A sense of uncertainty, and thus the potential for polysemic readings, is also set up from the opening shots on a close-up of an eye, a point-of-view shot of bamboo receding up to the sky, and a pull back and rotation of the camera to reveal a dishevelled man (Jack) dressed in a suit, lying dazed and bruised in the undergrowth. This is a common narrative device, pulling the viewer into the middle of some (as yet unknown) action. Who is this man? Where exactly is he? And why is he in this predicament? Does the fact that he pulls a miniature bottle of vodka from his pocket suggest that this is a 'morning after' scenario? If the viewer didn't know better from the publicity that this was a series about castaways, it might be just as plausible to deduce that the location was parkland somewhere in the USA, the yellow Labrador running past and the sneaker hanging on a bamboo cane doing nothing to subvert such an assumption. As he emerges from the bamboo grove onto the tropical beach and then runs through the burning wreckage of the plane, the *knowing* viewer has their expectations, primed from the trailers, met. Yet the juxtaposition, even at this early point signalling generic hybridity, is still jarring as the tracking shot moves from the idyllic lushness of the vegetation to the devastation on the beach with the sounds of cries and panic preceding the smoke and carnage.

Seen from Jack's narrative point of view at this point, he is quickly established as the hero and a man of action: he gives commands, rescues a casualty trapped under part of the plane, organises triage, administers CPR and urges survivors out of harm's way. 'I'm a doctor,' he says to Kate, indicating his status as an authority figure, and he stands up to the pain as Kate stitches him without anesthetic. The flashback to the plane crash (a single flashback in 'Pilot part 1' coming at the start of act two) is also recounted from Jack's point of view, and in it he is also shown as being in control, reassuring Rose who is disturbed by turbulence. However, when Kate remarks that he doesn't seem afraid at all, he talks of his fear, of learning to overcome it by giving into it, but only for a count of five. He is in command of his emotions, but he cries and has a heart too. Jack is also figured as romantic hero in his positioning with respect to Kate, who at the outset at least is positioned as his love interest, albeit an equally competent character. She is shown to be observant – spotting the smoke in the valley, and capable – stitching Jack's wound under his guidance. She volunteers to go and find the front section of the plane with Jack, takes hiking boots from a corpse, ventures into the cockpit – steeply angled against a tree, and goes back for Jack after the smoke monster attack. In terms of the latter, she is contrasted with Charlie, who appears cowardly, and is only there because he is in search of his drugs.

The main themes in season one are orientated around the establishment of such characters: who the survivors are and what lengths they go to while waiting for rescue or escape are used to define character types. As a group, they are depicted as pioneers, colonizing an alien landscape. In 'Pilot', Hurley is quickly established as helper and facilitator. Initially asked by Jack to assist the pregnant Claire, it is Hurley in the early episodes who sorts out useful items from the wreckage, distributes food, assists Jack in operating on Edward Mars, the US Marshal, and suggests doing something about the bodies. In later episodes he checks people against the manifest and sets up a golf tournament. He is also shown to be thoughtful, giving the pregnant Claire two airline meals on the first night after the crash. Similarly, Sayid in these early scenes is depicted as a technical strategist, building a fire to act as a rescue beacon and organising Charlie to help, repairing the transceiver, and leading the party to high ground to send a distress signal out. Subsequently, he undertakes his own exploration of the island, coming back with Danielle's maps. Other typical, if not stereotypical, characters are also introduced: the blonde 'bimbo' Shannon who is anxious to maintain her appearance and beauty regime, rock star Charlie with his antsy behavior (revealed to be due to his drug habit), the sardonic and selfish Sawyer who is depicted as anti-hero and later revealed as an emotionally-damaged con man, and the ominous Locke. Everyone has a role. As Sawyer says, 'Fine, I'm the criminal. You're the terrorist. We can all play a part.' Turning to Shannon, he adds: 'Who do you want to be?', suggesting at least that roles might be interchanged and conflated.

The seemingly straightforward character types (hero, heroine, helper, villain, anti-hero) are clearly more complex than they appear. As indicated by the Channel 4 trailer discussed in the introduction, the characters are enigma codes in their own right and are quickly established as part of the perpetuated hermeneutic. The details revealed about the characters frequently invite further questions about who they are; the flashbacks conceal as much as they reveal. All are hiding secrets – Charlie has an addiction, Kate is the murderer Mars was escorting back to the US, Sayid fought in the Iraq war on the 'wrong side', Hurley is a reluctant millionaire who believes he is cursed. Sayid, for example, is set up as an ambiguous character from the start, an Iraqi and a veteran of the Imperial Guard. Despite obviously wanting to put his role as a torturer behind him, he nevertheless reluctantly tortures Sawyer in an attempt to learn where Shannon's inhaler has been hidden. This impels him to turn his back on the group and set off on his own, whereupon he then himself becomes the tortured when caught by Danielle Rousseau. Repetitions and reversals such as this are commonplace and even when more about the character is revealed in flashbacks (the normal narrative function of the flashback), past events present further enigmas. As revealed in 1.9 'Solitary', not only is Sayid's background far more convoluted than might have been assumed, his very identity is also called into question. He tells his childhood friend and future love Nadia, a prisoner under interrogation, that this 'isn't a game', to which she replies: 'Yet you keep playing it, pretending to be something I know you're not.' Her reply suggests he may be cast in the role of the torturer but it is not his true nature. In this way, assumptions that might have been made about whether a character is 'good' or 'bad' are subverted. Similarly, Locke – who seems to faintly disgust Kate with his orange peel smile – has a scary collection of hunting knives and is positioned as a paedophilic threat to Walt (at least to Michael, and likely many viewers too) when he asks 'Walt, do you want to know a secret?'. Locke seems to be a particularly enigmatic character as he keeps a lonely vigil staring out to sea and revels in the tropical storm while everyone runs for cover, and later when he 'goes native' – hunting boar, claiming the island tells him what it wants, seeking to lead the Others, and ultimately 'becoming' the monster. In flashbacks, though, he is revealed to be a victim and a man struggling against the role life has apportioned him. The characters and their back-stories thus embody the perpetuated hermeneutic of the text and its many enigmas.

Complexity and ambiguity are also established via narrative point of view shifts with each episode, primarily via the associated character flashbacks (a complex form of unrestricted narration). The flashback is a standard drama format, relating the causal event of something happening in the plot and revealing more intimate details about the incident or character. Each episode focuses on a different character and off-island location, establishing the flashback as the dominant narrative structure of the series. But with each episode relating only a part of one character's life story, the viewer has to create a logical history. Moreover, sometimes the flashbacks have the appearance of objective storytelling, at other times there is an element of subjective memory. Throughout the 23 episodes of season one each of the main characters (Kate, Jack, Locke, Sun and Jin, Charlie, Sawyer, Sayid, Claire, Boone and Shannon, and Hurley) is the focus of at least one episode, with Kate and Jack both featuring in three. Revelations, sometimes introducing a dramatic twist, are made in these flashbacks, though they rarely provide resolution and later flashbacks are employed to subvert or make more nuanced elaborations. 1.4 'Walkabout', for example, is organised around the enigma of Locke. 'Who is this guy?' says Hurley on seeing Locke's knives. He is revealed as nothing like the hunter, or even perhaps serial killer, that the knives suggest though, and expectations are subverted. The flashbacks reveal him to be disabled and a wheelchair user. This explains both the presence of the chair amongst the luggage and the look he gives as he realises he can move his feet when he comes to after the crash (shown in the prelude of 'Walkabout'). However, the flashbacks tell us nothing about his 'condition' (maybe his recovery can be explained rationally) or about his identity beyond his stubbornness and determination (his rebuke 'Just don't tell me what I can't do' becoming a repeated motif). These aspects of the character will only be revealed later and do not always flow in a logical way (he is shown going through several moments of crisis with his father before the actual cause of the paralysis is revealed in 3.13 'The Man From Tallahassee').

While the flashbacks within any one episode for the most part relate to a single character (or couple in the case of Sun and Jin), they also interlink in increasingly complex and revealing ways as the series progresses. At the start of 'Pilot part 2', for example, a flashback depicts the moments preceding the crash from Charlie's point of view. This replays the same sequence as previously seen in 'Pilot part 1' from Jack's perspective and adds more detail to the viewer's overall knowledge of the crash. In Jack's flashback, Charlie is shown pushing Jack out of the way as he rushes past Jack's and Rose's seats. Charlie's flashback shows events before (his anxious tapping of his ring in the jungle after the pilot's death forms a bridge into the flashback where he is shown tapping the arm of his seat – he is, as the viewer will see momentarily, desperate for a fix) and after this point (as he runs from the flight attendants and takes his drug stash from his shoe in the toilet cubicle – this is where he is as the plane starts to go down and he has to drag himself to an empty seat in the mid-section). This adds detail to the crash event that will only be reconstructed as a whole across many episodes and several seasons and will include outside points of view – as with Desmond's role in causing the crash in 2.23/24 'Live Together, Die Alone' and with the Others witnessing it from the Barracks in 3.1 'A Tale of Two Cities' – and what happened at Sydney airport before the flight. In presenting multiple character viewpoints in this way (the narrative is both subjective and unrestricted) the series as a whole forms a jigsaw puzzle or mosaic, and viewers only begin to see the bigger picture as more pieces are added. This requires additional work and recall on the part of the viewer, but it is this perpetuated hermeneutic that has proved so appealing to the fan audience. In fact, some fans took the flashbacks of the crash and re-edited them into linear sequences. One example even includes excerpts from cut scenes in the *Lost* video game *Via Domus*.[6] In addition to the character-driven flashbacks, the flashforwards, time travel to earlier periods, and flash-sideways used in later seasons mean the perpetuated hermeneutic of *Lost* is extremely complex.

As Marc Oromaner states: 'The storyline [...] is basically a gigantic jigsaw puzzle, with every episode being a new piece to help reveal the overall big picture' (2008:

43). Moreover, it is these puzzle pieces that frequently encode the generic shifts from reality drama into telefantasy and science fiction. Among the puzzle pieces introduced in the first season are Locke's recovery from paralysis and what the island has to do with it, what kind of power Walt possesses that allows him to apparently bring pictures in books to life on (the polar bear) and off (the bird in Australia) the island (this makes him special in the eyes of the Others), whether Christian Sheppard is ghost or figment, who is whispering and what is being whispered, how can Rose possibly know for certain that her husband is still alive, what is the meaning of Hurley's cursed yet seemingly random numbers, what and – given the light that comes on when Locke requests a sign – who is inside the hatch? This narrative jigsaw draws the viewer in, not only by subverting expectations (and thereby constantly keeping viewers on their toes), but by creating an endless array of new questions arising from each revelation. Joley Wood (2007: i) provides a perfect example of this continual shifting of meaning when she asks, 'How does smoke stomp?'. The enigma of the black smoke begins with sound and movement effects that suggest an unseen creature. But *Lost* undermines any straightforward expectations in 1.24 'Exodus part 2', revealing the monster as something out of 'weird science'. Despite its nebulous form, the smoke can drag Locke away and pull him underground. Although characters have encountered the monster up close prior to this, it has remained an unknown to the viewer. If characters have seen it, then they either cannot comprehend what it is (Jack) or do not wish to acknowledge this (Locke). The appearance of the monster thus remains an enigma until the final episode of season one. Not only do the characters (or the viewer) not know how it stomps, but in addition they do not know what it looks like, what it is, where it comes from, or how it operates. They have no frame of reference. Even when informed that it is a security system or Cerberus (and thus a watchdog), this is hardly an explanation at all; what or who is it protecting, who if anyone is in control of it (in 3.15 'Left Behind', Juliet says that 'We don't know what it is, but we know that it doesn't like our fences' and in 6.16 'What They Died For', Ben says that although he was told he had a way to summon the monster, he has come to realise that 'it was the one summoning me'). In 'Exodus part 2', Locke wants the monster to drag him underground, believing he is being tested. Taken together with his endeavors to break into the hatch, this suggests the answers are under the ground, literally and figuratively buried. Jack intervenes, and the answers are delayed and ambiguous, as they are frequently throughout the series. In fact, opening the hatch adds major new mysteries to the series, not least around Desmond's role and the DHARMA Initiative operations on the island. As Orson Scott Card (2006: 11) asks: 'once *Lost* reveals its secrets—what really is happening on the island, what's it all for—what are they going to do?' The point is, that *Lost* never quite reveals any of its secrets. Within the perpetuated hermeneutic of the telefantasy series, answers must constantly be delayed and further enigmas introduced (also among these are the electromagnetic force, the seemingly ageless Richard Alpert, and the ability to physically move the island). The island itself is part of the perpetuated hermeneutic of course, but in forming a map or territory that must be explored it is also a major element of the hyperdiegesis.

Narrative as Map

Within the hyperdiegesis of *Lost*, the beach is quickly established as the central locale from which all other parts of the island extend. The opening sequence of 'Pilot' establishes the beach as a 'foothold' in what is *terra incognita*. The beach is the one place that remains static throughout the series. It signifies home; even in season five when Sawyer, Juliet, Miles and Daniel are time-jumping, they keep returning to it even when they are at a point before the camp has been established and at a time when it is abandoned and falling apart. The beach (initially at least) represents hope and salvation. As the ideal location for Sayid's rescue beacon, it is a signal point that will draw the attention of rescuers from across the sea. Shannon, perhaps the most desperate of the survivors to be rescued as she tries to maintain her self-image, remains on the beach alongside Kate, Sawyer and Sayid when Jack's party moves to set up a long-term base in the caves (1.6 'House of the Rising Sun').

The beach, however, is also a narrow fringe between the ocean on one side and the jungle on the other. It is a liminal space, the boundary between the terrors inland (where the monster that rips the pilot from the cockpit stomps) and the dangers of the sea (where Joanna, one of the survivors, drowns when she is caught in a riptide whilst swimming in 1.5 'White Rabbit'). Interior and exterior are both unknown territory. The dimensions, size and shape of the island are indefinite, the lush vegetation on the margin of the beach concealing what is beyond – it is not impenetrable but it is dense. The ocean is also an ambiguous space, unknowable in its vastness. As the pilot says, 'We were a thousand miles off course. They're looking for us in the wrong place.' The ocean is the route to safety – it is where they look for rescue – but it is also a barrier, fencing them in and keeping them lost. There are suggestions too that the beach is liminal in the sense of the safety it offers being illusory. When Jack worries about Kate's decision to go to high ground with Sayid to attempt an SOS call on the pilot's transceiver, she asks him 'What makes you think we're any safer here than we are in the jungle?' Nowhere is an ideal location, and the safety of the beach and also the caves with the spring (after Jack is led to them by the ghost of his father in 1.5 'White Rabbit') is fragile. In fact, the beach is unstable, and the first camp must be moved due to high tides and erosion (1.12 'Whatever the Case May Be'), while the cave is subject to rock falls (trapping Jack and Charlie in 1.7 'The Moth'), as well as being the place where Claire is attacked – Shannon refers to it as the 'rape caves' (1.10 'Raised by Another').

Conversely, the beach and the sea both demand to be explored and exploited. They offer sustenance – fish and sea urchins, various fruits, the boar, and eventually Sun's garden – and are gateways to the rest of the island. The narrative is structured around a number of explorations, each one adding to a cartography of the island, and these guide both the characters and the viewer. Many narrative developments in *Lost* are organised around journeys and routes radiating out from the beach: up the valley to find the cockpit, to the high ground to send a distress signal, into the jungle to search for luggage (when Kate and Sawyer find the waterfall), to hunt boar (and stumble across the hatch), to trek around the coastline (as Sayid does, whereupon he also follows the buried cable to one of Danielle's traps and her dugout), to sail away on the raft, to get the dynamite from the Black Rock, in pursuit of Danielle when she kidnaps Aaron, and as directed by ghosts and visions (Jack to the caves by the appearance of his dead father and Locke to the drug smugglers Beechcraft by a dream). The trek to find the cockpit in 'Pilot' is thus only the first in a sequence of excursions or quests, each adding information to the map and thus the hyperdiegetic world the characters inhabit. What is revealed of the island, though, always suggests further undiscovered areas, some of which are sophisticated experimental science stations, and evidence of occupation. The cable Sayid finds must feed power to something under the sea, the hatch indicates a sophisticated installation underground, Danielle's distress signal comes from a radio tower somewhere on the island, and Ethan's presence amongst the survivors suggests the island is in fact inhabited, as does Danielle's warning about the Others. As the series progresses, the storyworld expands into an increasingly complex geography: Desmond and the Swan Station, the other DHARMA Initiative stations, the second group of survivors from the tail section, the Others and the Barracks, the Hydra island, the donkey wheel, the three-toed statue, the Temple, the Lighthouse, and the cave on the cliffs.

Through its depiction of complex character and location interactions, *Lost*, as Sara Gwenllian-Jones has argued of the cult series generally (2004: 64), invites viewers into an intense imaginative engagement with the storyworld. The viewer is invited to map their own island, and indeed many have done so. Given the emphasis on maps within the text, it is understandable that real-world fan cartographers would attempt such an undertaking,[7] this being just one example of the creative speculation that the hyperdiegesis has generated. Projects such as these are aided by the provision of maps featured within the text. When Sayid returns from Danielle's dugout, he has her maps and notes (1.12 'Whatever The Case May Be'). Other diegetic maps include Ben's maps showing routes to the radio tower and to the Temple, Daniel's map showing the Tempest station, and Radzinsky and Inman's blacklight map that Locke discovers painted on the blast doors in the Swan during the lockdown incident (2.17 'Lockdown'), as well as a number of other sketch maps such as those made by Arzt plotting where the baggage might have fallen, the map Ben (masquerading as Henry Gale) draws to show the location of the balloon, and the one the Man in Black gives Sawyer in order to find the dock on the east coast.

Maps are thus important in offering the viewer a way to understand and interpret the spatial geometry of *Lost*. Such maps can show the way, but in the tradition of early maps there are always unexplored spaces within the diegesis. Danielle's maps (figure 2) are significant in this context. They are a literal and figurative jigsaw puzzle. Constructed across several sheets of paper, it is only when they are arranged in a certain way that Danielle's triangulation begins to make sense to Sayid. Her notations

Figure 2: Danielle's maps offer clues to locations on the island (episode 1.14 Special © ABC)

are drawn across the boundaries of several sheets and it is only when they are put back in the correct order that they can be understood. In 1.14 'Special', Sayid hypothesises that her directions are to the location of the transmitter, or perhaps the black rock (which at that point in the narrative, and given that the only references are in Danielle's account of returning from it with her team when first shipwrecked and in Claire's diary entries which refer to it only as something she has dreamt about, is assumed to be a geographical feature). The maps are incomplete though, and cannot be fully understood since they contain information beyond their geography. Sayid cannot understand this since he thinks only analytically. He attempts to understand Danielle's mathematical equations by translating her notations: A des reflets d'argent / La mer des reflets changeants. Shannon's translation (the sea of silver sparkles that change) is incomprehensible because the equation it is linked with is 'completely different, it doesn't relate'. He believes that another should 'say something about latitude or longitude, something about the stars', but it refers only to 'blue infinity'. These lines only appear to be nonsensical, however, and it is Shannon's recognition of them as lines from the song 'La Mer' that reveals the notations to be a reflection of Danielle's mental state as a bereaved mother. They are in fact part of an emotional and psychological journey, not a physical one. As Shannon says: 'Did you ever think that after sixteen years on mystery frickin' island your friend might not be quite adjusted?', and – once made sense of as song lyrics – indicate Danielle's sense of loss and her yearnings for her stolen child. These maps also chart a state of mind.

The island is thus the terra incognita of the unconscious. In 1.23 'Exodus part 1', Danielle refers to *territoire foncé* (dark territory) and it is where she takes them to find the Black Rock (the name of the ship also signifying a dark place). In her maps and notes it is *l'endroit le plus dangereux* (the most dangerous place). This area is labelled on the blast door map as 'Primary nexus of Cerberus related activity', and it appears to be the area where the black smoke 'lives'. The text refers to map locations, but the map itself is always incomplete. It is like the ancient map decorated with fantastical creatures and the mythic legend 'here be dragons'. The map on the blast door harkens back to such unmapped territory on antique maps with the Latin phrase *hic sunt dracones* being inscribed under a notation 'The Pearl?'. In fact, the island does contain the equivalent of dragons. In 'Pilot', when the survivors are first alerted to something in the jungle, it is with just a sound and the impacts of the monster on its environment – falling trees and a strange, almost mechanical noise. At this point, it is just an unseen force and could be potentially anything, though a viewer's knowledge of science fiction movies might lead them to conclude that it is some gigantic beast, that the survivors are in *Godzilla* (1954) or *Jurassic Park* (1993) territory. Hurley even hypothesises dinosaurs in 1.3 'Tabula Rasa'. Though such fears are dismissed (because, as Jack says, dinosaurs are extinct), they are what anyone with cultural knowledge of these films and their sequels, as well as *King Kong* (1933), *The Lost World* (1960) and *The Land That Time Forgot* (1975) might imagine. What other creature might seize a man from the cockpit of a plane and leave his corpse suspended high up in the branches of a tree? Certainly, there are other exotic and dangerous creatures out of time and place here: the polar bear, the boar, genetically-engineered 'hy-birds' with 16-foot wingspans. Given the other mysteries of the island, it is within the range of possibilities that this could be an isolated stretch of land where dinosaurs continue to thrive.

In introducing such mysterious and fantastical phenomena, the island is marked as uncanny. The sounds of the island itself are strange, for example. The 'monster' roars in a way that is not wholly animalistic, the sounds have a metallic clang and hum with a mechanistic edge. Charlie describes it as 'weird' as it is happening and afterwards Michael says that: 'It didn't sound like an animal – not exactly, I mean.' Charlie tries to explain it away as monkeys, to which Sawyer sarcastically replies 'Sure, it's monkeys. It's Monkey Island!' This ironic reference to a computer game series does not dispel the uncanny sensation that the event creates; perhaps it *is* King Kong or Gojira, and this is Skull or Monster rather than Monkey Island). 'Whatever it was,' Michael concludes, 'it wasn't natural', while Rose thinks that 'there was something really familiar about it'. This notion of the sound being both strange and strangely familiar suggests that the island is *unheimlich* and this is exacerbated by the fact that the monster is unseen, trees move and victims are seized but without sight of any creature – it is a spectral presence and remains so even after it is revealed (it is smoke and therefore lacks solidity).

Accordingly, the attack by the monster is shot like a horror film. Charlie says that the monster has a 'gargantuan quality' after it kills the pilot. It is also significant that this sequence (after the attack in the cockpit) also contains overhead shots of Charlie falling down, suggesting the monster's point of view with Charlie as victim. There are also stylistic elements here of the zombie or the slasher film, as well as the giant monster movie. When Kate is hiding in the banyan tree there is a palpable sense of being under threat. She counts from one to five just as Jack told her he had when he overcame fear during an operation – she too is scared. A moment later, Charlie in fact surprises her, a form of misdirection also common from the horror film. Moreover, shots framed by foliage are frequent in the first few episodes of season one, suggesting a voyeur, that the survivors are being watched from their first moments on the island. In one sense, this is revealed to be the case when Hurley works out that Ethan is not on the plane's manifest (indeed, it is later revealed that Ben Linus sends Ethan and Goodwin out to infiltrate the two groups of survivors from the middle and tail sections of the plane). But there is also a frequent suggestion of being watched with the whispering that is introduced in 1.9 'Solitary'. Danielle tells Sayid that she has never seen anyone on the island but she has heard them whispering and the sound is also heard by Sayid as he returns to the caves, and by Sawyer in 1.16 'Outlaws' when he is chasing the boar that is terrorising him. These whisperings re-occur more frequently throughout seasons two, three and four, and the over-riding suggestion of this is that there are indeed other people or creatures just out of sight in the vegetation. Where sense can be made of the whispering – as when Sawyer hears it and it includes the repeat of the line 'It'll come back around', Frank Duckett's last words when Sawyer shot him in the mistaken belief he was the con man who had caused his parents' deaths – it suggests uncanny knowledge. But the whispering has an eerie quality in its own right, and invites comparison to the monsters from the id of *Forbidden Planet* (1956). Although it is used to prefigure the Others during season two, it is also associated with the smoke monster. It occurs, for example, on the two occasions when Walt appears to Shannon dripping wet and speaking backwards, and just before Eko stares into the heart of the monster (and the camera moves through the smoke to show flash-frames of images from Eko's life). These scenes are constructed in such a way as to create uncanny moments within the series and imbue it with elements of paranormal horror.

Exposed, beset by monstrous entities, and literally lost in a wilderness, the crash survivors are not only explorers in an unknown land, but also victims in an uncanny tale of the paranormal. Each physical trip they make pushes back the boundaries of their (and the viewers') knowledge, but is also a journey into the unknown. These geographies of the island and life beyond it aid the development of a rich hyperdiegesis and add to the perpetuated hermeneutic. As Card points out: 'All these mysteries work together to create the overall thread of the story, the mystery that holds it all together' (2006: 14). Exhibiting the narrative attributes of the cult television series, *Lost* is arguably an important example of telefantasy and a highly engaging series that appears designed to produce creative speculation. This speculation extends beyond the television narrative into forms of transmedia storytelling that mark *Lost* out as a key moment in the history of convergence culture (see chapter 6).

Chapter 2: The Hatch

The narrative traits of *Lost* set out in chapter one (the perpetuated hermeneutic and the hyperdiegesis), in combination with the narrative complexity that invites interaction with the *Lost* storyworld, mean that *Lost* is an example of what Angela Ndalianis refers to as neo-baroque aesthetics (2005: 90). The 'rhythmic and polycentric organisation' of the neo-baroque series, characterised by story arcs and multiple storylines, is continuous across many episodes and carries over between seasons. Connections between episodes are pronounced and narratives not only develop stories from past episodes, but also rely on 'the active engagement of the audience familiar with prior episodes'. Such viewers recognise the 'virtuosity' of the series in constructing a multi-layered narrative based on variations on a theme (Ndalianis 2005: 95). Ndalianis argues that there are five progressive prototypes of the neo-baroque series, and the culmination of these is the series that that has no stable, singular, linear framework. Such series are 'riddled with multiple narrative formations that stress polycentrism' (Ndalianis 2005: 96). As an example of the neo-baroque, *Lost* not only interweaves multiple plot threads that continue over many episodes and even whole seasons, but frequently presents these in a highly fragmented way. The opening episodes of season two, for example, present material out of temporal order, replaying the same period of time from different character points of view. In 2.1 'Man of Science, Man of Faith' events are depicted immediately after the hatch is opened. Life in the established island locales around the caves and the beach is shown from Jack's perspective. The episode climax depicts Jack entering the hatch in search of Kate and Locke (who have done so earlier) and ends with him recognising Desmond (who has a gun pointed at Locke's head) from an earlier off-island meeting at a sporting arena. Episode 2.2 'Adrift' then takes place during the same period of time, relating simultaneous events taking place elsewhere and to other characters. It reveals what happened to Kate and Locke when they entered the hatch and also what happened to Sawyer, Michael and Jin after they were attacked by the Others and Walt was kidnapped (taking up from the climax of season one). The survivors from the tail section of the plane are also introduced for the first time in 'Adrift', and in 2.7 'The Other 48 Days' the time period of season one is replayed in order to fill in their part of the overall story. This temporal re-ordering is not integrated into the narrative, as the flashbacks are, in order to tell the personal histories of the characters. Rather the material is organised in a way that fills in gaps in the narrative. Moreover, this structure itself reflects the increasingly central science-fictional themes of time travel and alternate timelines in the narrative. The neo-baroque aesthetic thus serves the function of generic coding (in a sense, it is 'timey-wimey' in the way that *Doctor Who* has since further exploited). In this way, the viewer's understanding of the series, its characters, and the causes of certain events may be disrupted and the overall story reconstructed.

As this suggests, putting the whole story together into a logical whole is like completing a jigsaw puzzle. To quote Ndalianis (2005: 96-97), this requires the viewer 'to function like a puzzle solver or labyrinth traverser'. In the neo-baroque narrative, the viewer has to piece together multiple and divergent story fragments; in terms of transmedia storytelling, this also requires co-ordination of multiple interrelated plot fragments across different media. It is fitting that the complex fictional world of *Lost* is organised around recurring motifs of games and puzzles.

The Games in *Lost*

The puzzles of *Lost* – the numbers, the button, the hieroglyphics, the black smoke, the DHARMA Initiative stations, the orientation films, and the candidate list – provide a focus for the neo-baroque aesthetic. In keeping with these enigma codes, key elements of the narrative are frequently organised around games and game play. The way in which characters are configured as elements in a game is central to the meaning of the series. As revealed in episodes towards the end of the series, the island has been bringing ship-wreck and plane-crash victims to its shores for millennia (the Egyptians who built the three-toed statue, Jacob and the Man in Black's mother in the Roman era, the Black Rock slave ship, the French science team, and the drug smugglers in the Beechcraft). All of these survivors have been used as pawns in an endless battle of good and evil. It is as though the island is the game itself, and the people that wash up on its shores are the pieces in that game (the players being Jacob and his unnamed brother, the Man in Black).

Games are thus a defining motif, providing a link between the multiple storylines. In general, games become the means by which the survivors stave off boredom, forget their anxieties about being rescued, and gamble for scarce commodities. Hurley organises a golf tournament with clubs salvaged from the wreckage and makeshift balls (1.9 'Solitary'), the playing cards retrieved from the Swan are used by Sawyer, Kate and others in games of poker, and Jack outplays Sawyer at Texas Hold'em to win the medical supplies (2.17 'Lockdown'). It is Locke, however, who is established early on – with the backgammon set – as the character most strongly linked to games. 'Do you like to play games, John?' Jack asks him during the retrieval of the dynamite from the Black Rock in 1.24 'Exodus part 2'. As Locke handles the dynamite, he refers to the board game Operation: 'I always got nailed on the funnybone,' he says jokingly, and in an added touch of black humour he makes a buzzing sound as he lifts a stick. Confirming Jack's assumption, he simply replies: 'Absolutely.' This linking of the deadly serious (the dynamite being needed to blow open the hatch so the survivors have a safe retreat from the Others and Arzt having been blown to pieces in the mission) to entertaining pastimes (he is also shown doing a crossword puzzle in 2.8 'Collision', filling in the answer 'Gilgamesh' – a connection to Sumaria that is significant in the context of other games central to the *Lost* text) sets him up as someone who is not only accepting of his role on the island, but willing to take risks against the odds. He knows the danger of the dynamite, but also believes that there is a purpose to the island and its destiny for him; he will not die.

During a key scene in 1.2 'Pilot part 2', Locke's association with the opposing pieces of a board game is introduced. He has retrieved a backgammon set from the wreckage and is approached by Walt who is curious and asks if it is like checkers. Locke holds up a black piece and a white piece, telling Walt that it is a game of 'Two players. Two sides. One is light... one is dark.' This works to set up the key narrative opposition of the series, though it is not revealed until much later that this antinomy is embodied by Jacob and the Man in Black (and their proxies). It recurs at key points in the repeating motif of game pieces: the black and white stones with the 'Adam and Eve' skeletons in the cave in 1.6 'House of the Rising Sun', when Locke – with Tarot cards – appears to Claire in a dream, one eye solid black and the other white in 1.10 'Raised by Another', and in the game that the Man in Black finds washed up

Figure 3: The black and white game pieces found by the Man in Black (episode 6.15 Across the Sea © ABC)

on the beach in 6.15 'Across the Sea' (figure 3). Locke's explanation of backgammon to Walt also encompasses notions of the past (and thus links to the fact that similar sets of events are played out time and time again, as a board game would be). As revealed towards the end of the series, the island is the place where an eternal battle between light and darkness is being enacted. By telling Walt that 'backgammon is the oldest game in the world' and that 'their dice were made of bones', Locke makes a link to both the origins of civilisation (and thus human life) and to bodily remains (its opposite, death).

He elaborates thus: 'Archeologists found sets when they excavated the ruins of ancient Mesopotamia. Five thousand years old. That's older than Jesus Christ.' In fact, the root of backgammon to which Locke refers is the Royal Game of Ur. This is also very similar to Senet, a game that originated in Egypt, and this is the game the Man in Black finds on the beach. The Royal Game of Ur and Senet, as well as other similar games known to exist around the Mediterranean and in India, are considered to have been played in a similar way to backgammon, if not to be precursors to the contemporary game (Craig 2002: 167-8). The game is also linked to funereal rites and may have taken on more ritualistic meaning in later Egyptian culture. According to Wolfgang Decker (1992: 6), it probably took on 'symbolic significance related to the resurrection of the dead'. Pictorial depictions of the game have shown a player competing against an invisible opponent (Craig, 2002: 35). Indeed, it is a common trope of horror and fantasy for a character to play a board game with a god or death itself, usually for their life, with the most famous example being Ingmar Bergman's *The Seventh Seal* (1957). It can be argued that the Man in Black takes this role in *Lost*: he plays Jacob but insists on his own rules, he leaves the game pieces for his mother to find before he kills her, pieces are left with their corpses in the caves, and a set of scales in the cliff cave to which he takes Locke weighs black and white stones (recalling the way Anubis would weigh the hearts of the dead or the soul would be weighed at the Last Judgement). Senet and backgammon are also games in which the players race around the board to finish first, and the concluding episodes of *Lost* (which also focused on Jacob and the Man in Black's games) become a race of life and death. The contest between Locke (possessed by the Man in Black) and Jack (ordained as the new protector by Jacob) plays out over the light at the Heart of the island. According to Mother in 6.15 'Across the Sea', this is the source of life, death and rebirth. Given the Sumerian and hieroglyphic engravings on the stones in the Heart, it presumably predates the early Egyptian or Mesopotamian inhabitants of the island. Desmond has to pull the plug because this is the only way the story can come to an end – the fight between Jack and Locke on the cliff edge, and the death of Locke, forming an endgame to the series. Though crucially, in the context of the neo-baroque narrative, this is not actually the end, Jack having to reinsert the stone and restore the light to the heart of the island, whilst also making Hurley the island's new protector. Furthermore, in the transmedia narrative, the DVD box set for season six contained a 12-minute epilogue, 'The New Man in Charge'. Despite it being an endgame to Jacob and the Man in Black's, as well as Locke and Jack's, story, narrative closure is still not achieved.

Craig also points out that cuneiform tablets from Babylonia indicate that the Royal Game of Ur was also used as a form of fortune-telling. Landing on one of the rosette squares on the board was considered a sign of good luck, the middle square was referred to as the Square of Rebirth, and the twenty-seventh square represented water, which was to be avoided (Craig 2002: 35). Both rebirth and water are recurrent motifs in *Lost*. Several characters go through literal and figurative rebirths. Locke and the Man in Black are both 'reborn' as semi-permanent forms of the smoke monster, as are Christian Sheppard, Alex Rousseau, Richard Alpert's dead wife Isabella and Eko's brother Yemi. Jack and Charlie are also figuratively reborn when they emerge from the ground after the cave-in (1.7 'The Moth'); for Charlie especially this is significant since he is also emerging from his drug addiction. The episode title and the repeated motif of the insect and the cocoon within the episode (Charlie sees it in the cave and after he has thrown his remaining drugs onto the fire) suggest transformation and rebirth. This allows observant viewers to make intertextual connections to other science fiction texts that develop discourses of mutation and transformation in similar ways. Delenn's rebirth from a cocoon in *Babylon 5* (1993-98) is particularly apt – especially, perhaps, for science fiction fans since the actor Mira Furlan, who played Delenn, plays Danielle on *Lost*.

The rebirth discourse also opens up a religious intertext. Locke asks Charlie three times to destroy his heroin, referencing the Christ myth. Intriguingly, Charlie asks during this episode, 'Who needs a broken-down *rock god* on an uninhabited tropical island?' (my italics). Similarly, water plays a significant part in Charlie's death and in Sayid's resurrection. Sayid, fatally shot during the mission to detonate the Jughead nuclear bomb, seemingly returns to life after being immersed in the waters in the Temple (though Dogen and Lennon's tests suggest his body has been possessed, what Danielle refers to as 'infected'). The Heart of the Island itself is both accessed via water (it lies beyond a stream and a waterfall, and the stone that retains the light is beneath a pool of water) and also the source of water (it is this water that is in the Temple pool where Dogen immerses Sayid, carried there through ducts from the Heart). Furthermore, Charlie sacrifices himself when deactivating the jamming signal in the Looking Glass station, subsequently appearing to Hurley off the island. It is Charlie's fate to die by drowning. When Desmond is 'tasked' with saving his life again and again, only one of these potential deaths is by drowning (3.08 'Flashes Before Your Eyes') but it is given added significance in the context of Charlie's dreams in 2.12 'Fire + Water'. In the first of his dreams, Charlie cannot save Aaron as the baby is carried out to sea in his piano. In the second, he dreams that he has to swim out to sea to rescue Aaron. When he awakens he is actually standing in the waves holding the baby. Although he is blamed for trying to harm Aaron, the symbolism of the dream – Hurley, Claire and Charlie's mother form a tableau from Verrocchio's 'The Baptism of Christ' (which also appears on the wall in Charlie's childhood home) – equates him with the Christ figure. The link with baptism as a form of rebirth is followed through as Eko baptises Claire and Aaron. This is not necessarily to argue that Charlie is a straightforward Christic figure, but clearly the themes of destiny and salvation play out in his death. It is true to say he makes a knowing sacrifice by volunteering to go to the Looking Glass, but Desmond's interventions in his previous 'deaths' suggest Charlie is also a game piece with a particular purpose.

The Game of *Lost*

Although gameplay and Manichean themes are not unique to science fiction, both are familiar to viewers with cultural competencies in the genre; for example, with tri-d chess and Romulan pixmit cards in *Star Trek*, and the religious coding of the Force in *Star Wars*. In this way, the neo-baroque aesthetic draws attention to the underlying science fictional tropes of game play and destiny in the text. Moreover, discourses of fate, destiny, coincidence and luck are frequently linked to scientific and technological devices. In 2.9 'What Kate Did', Locke splices the film footage from the Swan with the reel secreted inside a Bible in the bunker used by the tail section survivors. He ponders what the odds are of finding the exact pieces needed to complete the Swan orientation film. 'I mean, think about it,' he says, 'somebody made this film. Someone else cut this piece out. We crash, two halves of the same plane fall in different parts of the island, you're over there, I'm over here. And now, here's the missing piece right back where it belongs. What are the odds?' Eko is unconvinced that there is anything controlling events, advising Locke not to 'mistake coincidence for fate'. Characters are thus divided between those who believe and those who do not. The narrative opposition represented here by Locke and Eko is repeated on several occasions. Locke literally repeats Eko's line 'Don't mistake coincidence for fate' to Desmond in 3.15 'The Cost of Living', but reversing the meaning when Desmond suggests that it is quite a coincidence that tracking Eko – who has gone to find his brother's body – and the mission to use the monitoring station in the Pearl have one and the same destination. In 1.24 'Exodus part 2', Sun poses a similar question to Shannon: 'Do you think all this... all we've been through... do you think we're being punished?' for 'Things we did before. The secrets we kept. The lies we told.' Shannon stands in for the viewer here, wanting an answer to another mystery, to know if that were the case, who would be punishing them. Fate, says Sun, but Claire interjects, insisting that there is 'no such thing as fate'. It is significant that it is Claire who takes this stance, given the fact she has ended up on the island as a result of her consultation with the psychic Richard Malkin who advised her against the initial adoption of her unborn baby (and certainly Claire shows an interest in astrology). In 1.10 'Raised By Another', it could even be interpreted that fate intervenes to prevent her signing the adoption papers when two pens both fail to write. It is as a direct result of this that Claire follows Malkin's advice to go to Los Angeles on flight 815. Sayid and Kate (1.7 'The Moth') discuss the odds of surviving when the tail section broke off while they were still in the air and the mid-section had cartwheeled through the jungle. 'Yet we escaped with nothing but a few scrapes,' Sayid says, and then 'no one's that lucky, we shouldn't have survived.' Kate puts it down to 'blind, dumb luck', replying that 'sometimes things happen, no rhyme, no reason'. These frequent discussions of coincidence and fate emphasis the narrative antinomy at work, but they also position rational scientific thought against irrational belief in parapsychology. This evokes the narrative tension of *The X-Files*, an interesting parallel in light of the fact that J.P. Telotte refers to *Lost* as *The X-Files*' 'closest kin' (2008: 24). Further, some characters come to believe that an omnipotent hand is directing the characters. Since it is Locke who is the key figure linked to game players and game pieces, his speech in 'Exodus part 2' is significant:

> Do you really think that this is an accident? That we – a group of strangers – survived, many of us with superficial injuries? Do you think we crashed on this place by coincidence, especially this place? We were brought here for a purpose, a reason, all of us. Each one of us was brought here for a reason.

Fate and free will are configured here through the game strategies that structure the narrative: the hand of god and the hand of the gameplayer are conflated. Despite his being positioned as accepting of the destiny the island has for him, however, Locke is not an unproblematical figure. He is depicted as resisting his own limitations and the roles that others seek to place him in. The line 'Don't tell me what I can't do' becomes his catchphrase as he constantly seeks to assert himself and his rights (as he does, for example, when told he cannot take part in the walkabout due to his disability). In a pivotal scene from his youth (4.11 'Cabin Fever'), his teacher Gellert attempts to direct him towards a science career, seeing this as Locke's natural talent. But Locke wants to be the man of action: 'Don't you understand that things like science camp are the reason why I get stuffed into lockers?' he says, and 'I'm not a scientist! I like boxing and fishing and cars. I like sports!' Gellert tells him that: 'You might not want to be that guy in the labs surrounded by test tubes and beakers, but that's who you are, John. You can't be the prom king. You can't be the quarterback. You can't be a superhero.' He rejects that destiny, however, and seeks out the one that goes against his strengths but which he conversely feels is his nature. The island has given Locke the opportunity to be that man of action: hunting, tracking, at one with nature, taking charge of the Swan and entering the numbers, turning the wheel at the Orchid to fix time, and – potentially at least – taking up a role as a leader. He chooses to play the part the island offers him because it suits his own desires; nevertheless, he is as much a pawn as the other characters in the hands of the Man in Black.

The numbers (4, 8, 15, 16, 23 and 42) are also a repeated motif through which viewers can recognise the virtuosity of the text. They provide a set of numerical co-ordinates that are perhaps the most intriguing and dominant aspect of the series. They are the winning numbers on Hurley's (and Simms's – his fellow inmate on the psych ward – before him) lottery ticket; the serial numbers on the hatch; the numbers entered into the computer in the Swan; they were in the repeating transmission that led the French expedition to the island and subsequently are in Danielle's notes; they are on the odometer in Hurley's car; on Desmond's vaccine and the one given to Claire in the Staff; and ultimately they turn out to be the degrees of the candidates' geographical locations in the Lighthouse and the numbers of the candidates on the cliff cave wall. The numbers also crop up in various combinations: in Flight 815, which departs from gate 23 at Sydney airport; in the key code for the sonic fence around the Barracks; in the auction lot for the Black Rock's log book; in the log number of the video tape that Inman shows Sayid when he gets him to collaborate. In this way, they also represent the chance versus destiny antinomy. For Hurley, this is confusing and a signifier of his 'madness'; the numbers are everywhere because they are all part of his delusion. For Locke, they are a signifier of the island's plan for him. Thus, they are apophenic, allowing for patterns to be seen where patterns do not exist (Brugger 2001). They also reflect the opposition between fate and coincidence since – for the characters within the *Lost* universe – they allow for the possibility of denial of chance.

The map on the blast door seen in 'Lockdown' is another case in point. Within the text, it is occult, literally hidden. The map can only be seen under a very particular set of circumstances, the discovery of which is like working out the clues and solving the puzzle in a video game. In examples of extra-texual referencing, the blast door map also appears – with a second layer that is revealed under different lighting conditions – as part of the *Lost* video game *Via Domus*, and on the backs of the four *Lost* jigsaws. When all four jigsaws were completed and arranged together, a UV light shone on the wrong side would show additional details of the blast door map. Clearly, the use of maps as hidden clues is extremely significant not only to the text itself, but to the extra-textual merchandising and commodification of the series. This map, like Danielle's, is also an interesting example of both physical and subjective states. The blast door map is diagrammatic, the outline of the island is not a cartographic coastline, but a simplified octagon (like the DHARMA Initiative logo). It does not show natural landmarks and contours, but is a representation of the DHARMA stations around a central question mark. Like a treasure map with an 'X' to mark the spot, the question mark represents the Pearl video surveillance station. When this is discovered by Locke and Eko in 2.21 '?', a literal question mark is revealed from above, made by a circular area of salted earth with the drug smuggler's plane at the place where the dot would be (the hatch into the Pearl is beneath it). It can be presumed that Radzinsky and Inman had suspicions that they were being observed from this unknown (to them) installation and were the subjects of an experiment – hence its centrality in their map. This map is also heavily textual (the text is difficult to read from the scenes where it is shown in the episode but it has been reproduced with greater clarity on the back of the jigsaws and in *Entertainment Weekly* the day after the episode aired – clearly indicating awareness that the map was going to incite great interest among viewers). Like Danielle's maps again, the blast door map seems to contain cultural references which hint at a psychological state of mind. Amongst the notations, equations and Latin quotations are the phrases: 'The remedy is worse than the disease', 'I think therefore I suffer', 'K behaving strangely; can't trust; have to watch out', 'What did he fear?' and 'A sick man's dreams'. The jigsaw also includes the additional statements: 'What good is peanut butter and cereal without milk', 'Need more mac and cheese' and 'There is no sickness / Quarantine is a hoax'. Suspicion, doubt, disease and hunger are all alluded to here, and reflect the potential state of mind and mental decline that entering the numbers every 108 minutes for many years could induce. The duration of the assignment in the original DHARMA schedule was nearly 18 months (540 days according to the orientation film seen in 2.03 'Orientation'), but Inman could have been there for almost ten years – assuming he had been recruited in 1992 shortly before the purge. In any case, according to Inman, Radzinsky had eventually committed suicide – presumably due to the isolation, stress and probable sleep deprivation. The map and its notation may therefore be, like Danielle's, the ravings of a mind that is 'not quite adjusted'. It is as tantalizing as the lyrics in Danielle's notes, and might well be equally as meaningless.

The numbers and the games in *Lost* comprise a system of motifs, codes and symbols that lend the narrative complexity and depth, comprising a science fictional storyworld. This semiotics extends beyond the storylines themselves, encouraging the viewer to be drawn into a series of paratexts. This *Lost* experience is built around the wealth of material linked to and associated with the series, including the video game and jigsaws mentioned above, as well as the media coverage, merchandise, virals, other web material, computer and alternate reality games. Audience reception of the series has thus been largely structured around systems of signs, creating a rich semiotic field and a multi-layered polysemic text that conveys a sense of participating in game play for committed viewers, as much as simply watching a captivating series. Meaning is created through a set of key semio-narratological codes and these are explored in the following chapters.

Chapter 3: The Barracks

In keeping with the mapping of a geography of the island discussed in chapter 1, *Lost* also introduced various community groupings: the survivors of the plane's midsection who set up camp around the beach and the caves; the people already living on the island, usually referred to as the Others (sometimes the Hostiles or the Natives), who when they appear in season two are masquerading a primitive lifestyle (although Kate finds costumes in the Staff medical station that suggest otherwise); a second group of survivors from the tail section of the plane who came down on a beach on the opposite side of the island and took refuge in an abandoned bunker (the remaining members of this party after most had been killed or taken by the Others eventually joined the mid-section group); the DHARMA Initiative who built a series of scientific research stations across the island, though in the present of the island they are only seen on film and the only remaining link to this group is Desmond (although he is not a member of DHARMA); and Danielle, who has survived alone on the island for fourteen years. The various communities open up a number of key points about representations of identity, particularly in science fictional terms of the alien other.

The other is a foregrounded concept on *Lost* since the narrative point of view is constructed around the survivors (who are therefore 'us'), while the antagonists are even given the name 'the Others' (a very literal 'them'). In fact, the survivors of the tail section also refer to the people who are attacking and taking their members as 'Them'. Furthermore, in episodes set in the past when the DHARMA Initiative were active on the island, the original habitants of the island are referred to as 'Hostiles' – signifying this group as the violent other. As Stuart Hall (1997) has established, all cultures mark difference and this serves to stigmatise those outside the group and allow the members of that group to close ranks against these outsiders. *Lost*, however, twists its encoding of difference by reversing traditional viewpoints of antagonist and protagonist. A repeated motif in the series, for example, is a member of the Others telling the survivors that they are the 'good guys'. Ethan tells Claire they are good people and a good family (2.15 'Maternity Leave'), Ben says that Ana Lucia killed 'good people who were leaving you alone' (2.20 'Two For the Road'), and then tells Michael that 'we're the good guys' (2.23 'Live Together, Die Alone part 1'). This sows seeds of doubt about any straightforward meaning of the other in the series; as Hall argues, difference can be paradoxical in that it can potentially destabilise or unsettle social and cultural order (1997: 225-226). Such is the case with representations of gender in the series. While intersections of gender and class are notable in this respect, the oppositional positionings that arise from depictions of femininity and motherhood are significant, not least since they are related to science fictional themes of reproductive technology.

Gendering the Others

Figure 4: Juliet's book group creates an illusion of suburbia (episode 3.1 A Tale of Two Cities © ABC)

The title of the opening episode of season three, 'A Tale of Two Cities', immediately suggests an 'us and them' duality based around class and privilege. Charles Dickens's two cities are of course the two social classes that populate Paris – the aristocracy and the proletariat. Considering the way in which the opening of the episode reveals that the Others lead a suburban lifestyle (confirming that their primitive clothing, shabby appearance and crude encampment are a masquerade), they can be aligned with an elite class occupying a relative position of luxury compared to the survivors in their beach encampment (even with the resources from the Swan at their disposal).

However, there are more subtle and significant differences *within* the group that become clear in the opening sequence.

This sequence is notable in its own right. One facet of the neo-baroque aesthetic as discussed in chapter 2 is the introduction of new communities and characters via spatial and temporal dislocations in the opening sequence of each season (as with Jack's movement from the vegetation to the crash site in 1.1 'Pilot'). The opening sequences of both seasons two and three subvert expectations by seeming to be off-island flashbacks, but in the first instance is revealed as inside the Swan in the present, and in the second as the very recent past on another part of the island. But it is the latter that is particularly notable in terms of gender representation. It is constructed in such a way as to appear to be taking place in a suburban environment and opens with a very normal scene of feminine domesticity as a woman (Juliet) prepares her home for a book group meeting (figure 4). In the typical repetitive rhythms of the *Lost* narrative, this sequence begins with an extreme close-up of a woman's eye opening (mirroring that on Jack's eye at the start of 'Pilot'). Juliet plays a CD (dating this as any time from the early 1980s onwards since there is little else in the mise-en-scène to give a more concrete timeframe), composes herself in the mirror, arranges chairs, plumps the cushions on her sofa and rushes to the cooker when she realises she has burnt her muffins. This domestic space is thus coded as female-centric. An older woman guest (Amelia) arrives, and again there is nothing to suggest in the small talk that this is anything but a normal social situation. The exterior shots are medium close-ups and tightly framed so as to give the suggestion that the vegetation around the house could be garden shrubs and lawn, reinforcing the assumption that this is suburbia. Even though Juliet seems troubled or sad, such depictions of emotion are common in domestic drama and the soap opera, and may in any case be due to nothing more than being flustered at the imminent arrival of guests or the fact that a man is still working on her broken plumbing. In fact, as the cut to the next scene reveals, she is hosting a book group, again a very ordinary everyday event for the kind of middle class, suburban woman she appears to be. But a number of details break into this impression of normality.

The most obvious of these is the revelation at the end of the scene that the house is in fact on the island. The book discussion is interrupted by what might be assumed to be an earth tremor (this potentially confirming to the otherwise unknowing viewer that the setting is Los Angeles or elsewhere in California). But again, expectations are disrupted, just as they were when season two opened on scenes showing Desmond in the Swan. In that instance (2.1 'Man of Science, Man of Faith'), the sequences were shot in such a way as to suggest a flashback to the 1970s. The tight framing and close-ups on the mise-en-scène with old-fashioned fluorescent green cathode ray tube computer monitor, oval window beside a built-in table and benches that appear to be made from formica, other retro 70s-style furnishings and especially the foregrounding of the lava lamp and stainless-steel record player, the Mama Cass Elliot track 'Make Your Own Kind of Music' from 1969 all suggest this might well be the past. A similar disturbance to the apparent earth tremor during the book group interrupts the sequence with Desmond: a rumble (which could again easily be a small Californian quake) throws the needle arm across the vinyl record and Desmond rushes to put on some kind of uniform and operate a viewing device. A subjective tracking shot takes the viewer through a series of tunnels and shafts with observation mirrors to zoom in on Jack and Locke looking down the shaft – the twist, of course, being that the activities we have been observing are not taking place in some city like Los Angeles in the 1970s, but inside the Swan on the island now. Similarly, when the book group rush outside in 'The Tale of Two Cities', the man working on Juliet's plumbing is revealed to be Ethan (whom the viewer will recognise as the interloper who kidnapped Claire in season one), and Henry Gale (who was imprisoned in the Swan in season two) is shown leaving a neighbouring house. The viewer's assumptions are again subverted. Of course, the viewer is by now fully aware that the events they have been viewing are on the island, but the geographical location is emphasised by a series of aerial shots as the camera pulls back and up, cutting to wider and wider framed images revealing the location to be a village in a clearing in the jungle within a circle of mountainous peaks on the island. Trails of smoke in the sky lead down to two points either side of a promontory on the island. This is the crash of Oceanic flight 815, just 68 days earlier in the storyworld timeline, a time simultaneous with the opening episode of season one and with the electromagnetic force being released when Desmond failed to get back to the Swan in time to enter the numbers after following (and killing) Inman in 2.24 'Live Together, Die Alone part 2'. This single event forms a quilting point between the three seasons, filling in crucial information as Ben sends Goodwin and Ethan off to check if there are survivors and, if there are, to masquerade among them. This reinforces the oppositional nature of the Others even as it simultaneously humanises them.

It is significant in this respect that it is Juliet who is the primary point of view character amongst the Others in this sequence. The track Juliet selects as she gets ready for the book group is Petula Clarke's 'Downtown', a song intended to lift the listener's spirits, one that tells of burying one's loneliness and worries beneath the hustle and bustle of a city at night. Juliet pulls herself together to this track before the members of the book group arrive and this gives the impression that she has used the song in this way many times before. A suggestion that she is essentially unhappy is lodged in the mind, and will of course later be confirmed. Once it is revealed that Juliet's 'suburban' house is in the middle of open grasslands, one of a small cluster of cabins, on the island, the upbeat escapism that *Downtown* signifies is no longer possible. There is no way in which she can subsume her depression and loneliness in the liveliness, activity and bright lights of city nightlife, because there is no city and no nightlife here. Social groupings are a significant factor for those living on the island, class is implicit in this as established by the relative affluence of the Others' village compared with the survivors' makeshift encampments and subsistence lifestyle. But the positioning of Juliet makes it clear that gender is a point of difference too, both within the community and in contrast with the masculinity embodied by Desmond. Neither Juliet nor Desmond are in a place they wish to be, but in opposition to the loner hero Desmond, Juliet is both part of, and clearly marginalised within, the group. This is signified by her choice of book – Stephen King's *Carrie*, appropriately a novel concerned with a bullied and abused female character and about misunderstood feminine power. It is questioned by the apparently middle class, highbrow book group, especially the men in the group. 'It's not even literature,' says Adam, going on to call it 'popcorn', 'by-the-numbers religious hocum-pocum' and 'science fiction' (suggesting that the genre has no value within highbrow culture). In mentioning the absent book group member Ben, and implying the reason he is not present at the discussion is the choice of book, the suggestion is that Adam sees Ben as the arbiter of patriarchal cultural taste within the group (defining a hierarchy of taste with the masculine above the feminine).

This can be interpreted as representative of gendered differences. These are clearly set out in terms of cultural consumption, Juliet sarcastically apologising for 'sinking so low'. The relevant aspect of Juliet's choice of King, or of 'science fiction' as Adam classifies it (though perhaps most people would think of it as horror), is that it is considered low culture. Furthermore, women's tastes for genres such as romance and soap opera have been similarly positioned as oppositional and subordinate (Thornham 2007: 61). Ben and Adam's opposition to Juliet's choice references the demoting of feminine genres and female consumption in the hierarchy of cultural taste, whilst at the same time it can be interpreted from a feminist point of view as reclaiming women's culture and politics (Thornham 2007). Although the genres of fantasy, science fiction and horror are still to some extent considered masculine genres, these types of fiction (including King's work) have a large female readership. As Gary Hoppenstand and Ray Browne (1987: 5) point out, King's horror novels (including *Carrie*) are written specifically for a young adult and female readership. Indeed, *Carrie* seems an ideal choice by Juliet in terms of the representations of gender in *Lost*. In a flashback to when she was 10 years old (5.17 'The Incident part 2') Juliet's parents tell her they are divorcing. She does not understand why two people who love each other would not want to be together and takes the news badly, rejecting her mother's comfort and running out of the room. The implication that Juliet has a difficult relationship with her mother (and certainly the majority of characters on *Lost* have troubled relationships with their parents)[8] means that it is reasonable to assume that an adolescent Juliet found comfort, identification or catharsis in *Carrie*. The novel can also be linked to the adult Juliet and her conflict with the patriarchal hegemony on the island (although Ellie Hawking appears to have a leadership role amongst the Hostiles in the 1970s, the key leadership roles are all invariably filled by men). King has said himself that '*Carrie* is largely about how women find their own channels of power' (1981: 198), and whilst it cannot of course be viewed as unproblematically feminist, the novel can be read as a revenge fantasy. Juliet fills a similar function as a character to Carrie, eventually causing the deaths of men who have wronged her. Despite her relationship with Edmund Burke having ended, he is still – as her boss – a manipulative and controlling influence on her life. When Richard Alpert approaches her in 3.7 'Not In Portland' with the offer of a position at Mittelos Biosciences, she is concerned that Burke will not permit her to leave her current post. Alpert proposes reaching out to him on her behalf since there 'must be something that he would respond to', but her answer is to suggest that being hit by a bus would be the only thing that would work. When, just five scenes later, Burke is indeed hit by a bus, Juliet seems guilt-stricken that she wished it upon him. When Alpert approaches her in the morgue, though, he refers to it as a tragic accident that she cannot blame herself for. Given the many other instances throughout the series of seemingly random events being engineered by those from the island, it might not be too much of a stretch to read this seemingly chance event as having been arranged by Alpert. In the context of *Carrie*, however, it is not inconceivable that this could be read as Juliet's emotional state having triggered the incident. It is, after all, Carrie White's emotions – and her hormones – that trigger her telekinetic powers, and Juliet is shown in tears at the point she 'wishes' Burke would be hit by a bus. And when this happens, she is in a state of heightened excitement that her treatment has enabled her sister to conceive.

Although Ben is not present at the book group in 'Tale of Two Cities', his opinion is disclosed in 3.16 'One of Us', set on the day before the meeting. 'I was just finishing *Carrie*,' he says, adding that 'I still don't know why you picked it, but boy is it depressing…' Juliet does not respond to this, but Ben's comments can be read as illustrative of a class difference between Ben and Juliet, emphasising her marginalisation and outsider status (she is a recent recruit to the island). He also embodies the traits of an abusive masculinity; jealous of Juliet's relationship with Goodwin and claiming her as 'his', he engineers her lover's death (4.6 'The Other Woman'). It is clear from this and similar sequences that Juliet is being oppressed by Ben, who on many occasions appears to be a chronic liar and manipulator. In 'One of Us', Ben, in the role of coercive controller, flatly refuses to let Juliet go home. Even after three years on the island, Juliet still sees Florida and her family (significantly her sister, and thus representative of the wider notion of sisterhood) as home. Conversely for Ben the island, an embodiment of his leadership – and thus patriarchal – role, is home. It is the place he has chosen to be, siding with the Hostiles and taking part in the purge of DHARMA personnel, and is the only place he can be. In 3.20 'The Man Behind the Curtain', he tells Locke that he 'was born here on this island'. Although in a literal sense this is another of his lies – he was brought to the island as an 8-year-old when his father got a job with the DHARMA Initiative, it is also figuratively true. In 5.11 'Whatever Happened, Happened', Kate and Sawyer take the 12-year-old Ben to the Others after he has been shot by Sayid. Alpert says that if he takes him, 'he's not ever gonna be the same again. [...] His innocence will be gone. He will always be one of us.' He is reborn on the island. Regardless of the actual circumstances of his birth, Ben is one with the Others. Juliet on the other hand will never fully be one with this group and can ultimately be aligned with the survivors of Flight 815. It is therefore significant that, when defending her choice of book for the group to discuss, she refers to free will and of having the freedom to select a book that Ben wouldn't like. If nothing else, it is an act of feminine resistance and, symbolically, a re-negotiation of her place in the community.

Pathologising the Mothers

It is interesting in this representation of gender that Juliet is a fertility expert. As revealed in 3.7 'Not In Portland', she was recruited by Mittelos Bioscience to conduct research into preventing the deaths of pregnant women and their babies on the island. Juliet is thus a key figure embodying the gendered science fiction theme of reproductive technology. Various interventions in the processes of reproduction are a common theme of science fiction, including *Demon Seed* (1977), *Children of Men* (2006), and the *Alien* franchise (1979-). Following Donna Haraway's model of rational science (1991), Lisa Parks argues that *The X-Files*' Dana Scully is a monstrous figure since she articulates and negotiates scientific and technological discourses within a feminised body (1996: 122). In much the same way, Juliet's feminised body (and gender representation discussed above) embodies the rational science of reproductive technology. The fact that she is unsuccessful in saving the lives of pregnant women and their babies on the island, and thus represents a failure of medical science, is also a facet of the narrative opposition between reproductive technology and female biology. Claire is a pivotal character in this opposition, though other women on the island – Kate, Sun, Danielle – form a set of interconnected female characters representing motherhood.

The fact that Claire is eight-months pregnant when she comes to the island puts her and her baby at risk from the island's effects (ostensibly an autoimmune response connected with the electromagnetism). It is significant the Others' interventions to try and save the baby is coded in terms of an alien abduction trope, familiar from Scully's abduction, implant, cancer and pregnancy in *The X-Files* (Parks 1996: 124). Claire is positioned in the comparable role of abductee. She is kidnapped by Ethan, injected, rendered unconscious and amnesiac – and thus subject to fragmented memories similar to abductee accounts, and is implanted with a device that causes her to fall ill. Like Scully too, she later 'loses' her child – in both series the baby has to be raised by others to keep it safe. A prelude to this science fictional reading of Claire's story in 1.10 'Raised by Another' creates a horror atmosphere with her dream about the consequences of giving her baby away. The paranormal aesthetic is set up in the flashback of her visit to Malkin, a psychic, that ends when he refuses to reveal whatever horrific future he has seen in her palm. Subsequently, the night-time attack on Claire by an unknown assailant with a hypodermic needle resembles a scenario from a slasher film. And finally, Jack's diagnosis that she is imagining it – that she is a hysterical woman overcome by her pregnancy hormones – might have come from a psychological horror 'women's picture'. Nonetheless, the fact that Claire thinks the attacker injected her in the stomach introduces the notion of medical intervention.

It is the aftereffects of the abduction by Ethan, however, that move this storyline firmly into alien abduction territory. After being missing for a period of around two weeks, Claire returns to the camp in 1.15 'Homecoming' suffering from amnesia – a textbook example of lost time. Similarly, her returning memories in 2.15 'Maternity Leave' are also presented in a way that aesthetically resembles memories of experiments during an alien abduction. She even creates a screen memory, imagining she is at an obstetrician's surgery back in Australia prior to travelling to the US for an adoption. In fact, Claire is remembering being in the Staff. In her flashes of memory, shots focus on high tech medicine – the medical fridge full of vials, hypodermic needles, ultrasound equipment, a medical team in white gowns and caps preparing to operate, and clinical corridors. This creates an intertext with scenes of abduction in other science fiction media, not least *Communion* (1989). In 3.16 'One of Us', the parallels with Scully's (supposed) alien abduction scenario – an implant and cancer –

in *The X-Files* continues when Claire falls ill. The explanation Juliet gives is that Claire is suffering withdrawal from the serum that Ethan administered, a treatment Juliet developed to keep women alive during their pregnancies. This is revealed as a lie when Juliet subsequently contacts Ben; she has been sent to infiltrate the camp and gain the survivors' trust just as Ethan was earlier. Claire's illness is in fact caused by the triggering of the implant. Doubt is thus cast on Juliet's motivations; she will only transfer her allegiance later, and she is thus in a liminal position at this point. This confirms both Juliet as the embodiment of medical and reproductive technology, and Claire as alien abductee.

In further references to fears of pregnancy in science fiction and horror, 'Maternity Leave' creates heightened modes of emotional affect. Anxiety is generated by the obstetrician preparing a sedative, and by the fact this is out of place for a normal pre-natal examination. Indeed, Claire looks worried at this point, and for the viewer the anxiety is confirmed by a pull back to reveal that the obstetrician is Ethan. His supposed reassurance that he is giving her 'a little medicine for your baby' only raises more questions. Why does the baby need medicine? And when he injects her in the stomach saying 'it's a vaccine, we don't want him to get sick', the question is, a vaccine against what? Answers are not forthcoming, and beyond the fact this is an extension to the perpetuated hermeneutic, there is a clear subtext of (masculine) medical intervention in the normal processes of pregnancy. The contrast here between Ethan as assertive and commanding, but patronising, doctor, and the drugged Claire who is acting subservient and girly is strongly emphasised.

Further, in opposition to this masculinised depiction of medical technology, representations of feminine bonding through pregnancy and childbirth also centre around Claire. Claire is paired – and contrasted – with Kate on the one hand, and with Danielle on the other. In 1.20 'Do No Harm', Kate acts as midwife and doula. In the former role, with Jack preoccupied by other medical matters (of more import in terms of medical technology – setting up the equipment to give Boone a blood transfusion and then to amputate his leg), she assists Claire in delivering the baby. In the latter, she promises not to leave when Claire goes in labour, and when Claire expresses concerns that they (Ethan) did something to the baby and she can't love it, Kate persuades her that she can – and already does. Kate is thus positioned as the embodiment of feminine midwifery in opposition to Jack, who embodies masculine medicine with his heroic acts of life-saving doctoring; it is not insignificant that he fails in this in Boone's case. Women are therefore presented in terms of female bonding around childbirth, contrasting strongly with Jack's and Ethan's roles as perpetrators of masculine medical technology with its interventions in the normal process of childbirth and the medicalisation of pregnancy (and also the reason why the liminal Juliet is monstrous in Haraway's terms). Kate's centrality (Charlie is peripherally central too, which is permitted since he is not heroic or traditionally masculine and is willing to perform a caring, nurturing role with Claire and Aaron) is shown when all of the survivors gather around Claire and baby. The scene is a reminder that they are all one family, with the mother at its heart, but Kate is also standing with Claire in this grouping. This contrasts with her claim that she couldn't be a good mother (in 4.04 'Eggtown'). Claire's reply that she should 'try it sometime' presages Kate's role as foster mother to Aaron when the Oceanic Six leave the island. It also constructs a hierarchy of motherhood: Claire is the central mother-figure, Kate is next in line as midwife and later foster parent. Other women are positioned lower on this hierarchy. When Sun tries to give Claire advice in 2.15 'Maternity Leave', Claire counters by asking 'Are you a mother?' This suggests that Sun's advice is of less value and Sun herself, being childless, lower on the hierarchy (at this point Sun is pregnant but does not yet know it). This is further emphasised when Sawyer retorts, 'No boys allowed, huh?' – men are placed firmly below all women. This gender-normative hierarchy is problematised in a number of ways however, and not only by Charlie's nurturing, feminised role.

In particular, Kate is depicted as child-free by choice, and not 'childless' as Sun thinks she is, when she is shown to be ambivalent about motherhood. At this point in the narrative, there is a suggestion that Kate may in fact be pregnant, but it is conveyed via an 'is she or isn't she' teasing interplay with Sawyer. She does, however, follow through on Claire's suggestion of 'trying motherhood'. The 'Eggtown' conversation with Claire is linked to a flashforward showing Kate in the good mother role, refusing to use her son at her trial for the murder of her father, and thus protecting him. In what is a moment of reveal at the end of this flashforward, Kate's son is shown to be an older Aaron. Ultimately, though, Kate's mothering role is one she must relinquish.

In 5.11 'Whatever Happened, Happened', Kate loses Aaron in the supermarket. She is quickly reunited (Aaron has followed a woman who resembles Claire, emphasising the fact Kate is not his 'real' mother), but afterwards, she tells Cassidy – the mother of Sawyer's child – that she wasn't surprised. She took Aaron from Claire, therefore someone would take him from her. She defends her action on the grounds Claire was gone and had left Aaron already (having followed the Man in Black in the guise of Christian Shepherd into the forest). It is after this, that Kate gives Aaron into the care of his grandmother and returns to the island intending to rescue Claire. In one respect, this represents Kate wanting what is best for Aaron, but it is also part of the theme of mothers losing their children (men lose their children too – Michael loses Walt when the boy is kidnapped by the Others, for example, but this is often part of the discourse about difficult paternal relationships.)

As an embodiment of loss, Danielle is the opposite of Claire – the bereaved mother that counterpoints Claire's Madonna figure. When Sayid encounters Danielle in 1.09 'Solitary' she is a distraught PTSD sufferer constantly reliving the trauma of the Others taking her baby at one week old, an impression confirmed across her appearances in subsequent episodes. In 2.15 'Maternity Leave', Danielle's despair emerges as a desire for death. Although she killed her team because they were 'infected' soon after their arrival on the island, she cannot kill herself. 'Go ahead, please. Do it,' she says when Kate holds the gun on her during their unsuccessful mission to find vaccine in the Staff, adding that Kate was 'not the only one who didn't find what they were looking for.' Of course, Danielle is hoping to find her daughter Alex (who had helped Claire escape when Ethan was holding her there), but this stresses the parallel between Danielle and Kate (who should know what she must do if Aaron is infected – that is, kill him). Both women are here coded as outside the emotional attachments of motherhood – Danielle by her loss and Kate by her child-free status. More importantly, it also foreshadows Claire's reversal from Madonna to 'mad woman of the jungle', inheriting Danielle's role after she is separated from Aaron. The loss of the child is framed as a cyclical occurrence in 'Exodus part 1' when Aaron is a week old and Danielle claims the pillar of black smoke means the Others will take him from Claire (in fact, Danielle does). Danielle taking Aaron and leaving Claire distraught swaps her and Claire's roles. As Sayid says to Charlie in 'Exodus part 2',

'Don't try to apply reason to her actions, she's a mother who lost her child. Just like Claire.' The reversal is complete in 6.05 'Lighthouse'. Claire is dishevelled, living in a makeshift hut, making traps to catch Others, and with a bear skull substituting for her baby. Claire has become Danielle, obsessing over the Others whom she believes stole her child. This is not the case, but her unwavering belief that it is, even when Jin tells her Kate has Aaron, makes her connection to Danielle all the stronger.

Maternal bodies are thus a site of struggle in *Lost*. Juliet's opposition to Ben originates in a dispute over the maternal body, both her sister Rachel's (it is Juliet's treatment that has allowed her to conceive) and the island's pregnant women (whom she has been recruited to save). Claire's pregnant body is the subject of medical technology masquerading as alien abduction. Motherhood is associated with loss. Moreover, this theme is in keeping with the subtexts of *Carrie* that concern the maternal body, abjection and the monstrous feminine. While *Lost* does not depict the abject or the monstrous feminine in the same way as King's horror does, it nonetheless presents the female body and reproduction as problematical and therefore monstrous in the manner of Haraway's boundary creatures (1991). In this way, the social is linked to the technological through the semio-narratological codes. Additional representations of science and technology are explored further in the next chapter.

Chapter 4: The Freighter

As a postmodern hybrid text, *Lost* incorporates the conventions of many different generic formats. However, as addressed in chapter 3 in relation to reproduction, science fictional themes are employed in the series to convey a sense of anxiety within the storyworld. Lincoln Geraghty (2009) sets out how science fiction responds to and reflect historical and political concerns. Anxieties around nuclear weapons, the Cold War, the space race, civil unrest and computer technology are encoded into science fiction, and the genre pays constant attention to 'themes of science, technology, nature run amok, alien invasion, conspiracy, disaster and space exploration' (Geraghty 2009: 2). *Lost* similarly encodes the anxieties of the cultural moment: the black smoke is nature run amok, the polar bears and hy-birds are the result of genetic manipulation, and the Swan station is the means by which humans are enslaved to computer technology. As Paul Sutton states (2010: 63), the incorporation of science fiction into a series that is not straightforwardly science fiction allows it to deal with 'contemporary anxieties surrounding scientific advancement'.

More specifically in relation to *Lost*, Simon Brown (2010: 157) describes the generic concerns of cult television as 'conspiracy theories and SF'. When hybridised with more mainstream themes, telefantasy can be produced and marketed as mainstream drama with cult appeal. Drawing on the examples of *The X-Files* and *Twin Peaks*, Brown suggests that these leanings towards the mainstream are organised around the investigative procedural, but *Lost*'s anchoring references to populist cinema (*Cast Away*) and reality television (*Survivor*, 2000-) provide appeals to its mainstream viewers alongside the science fiction tropes that attract the fan audience. Whilst *Lost* does not engage with conspiracy theories directly, the enigmas that constitute the perpetuated hermeneutic are organised around shadowy companies, often with questionable aims or morals. Furthermore, the activities of these companies are frequently linked to themes familiar from the science fiction genre, namely time travel, scientists' ill-advised experiments with natural forces, and the end of the world. Whilst these narrative themes are often framed in ways that could equally be read as paranormal horror (they are often presented as miracles, premonitions and faith), they remain rooted in the genre of science fiction.

Mired in Conspiracy

Aspects of science and technology in *Lost* are primarily encoded in the representations of organisations and corporations, and the characters associated with them, including those involved in science-based experimentation, exploration and even commodification of the island. Chief amongst these organisations are the DHARMA Initiative, Mittelos Biosciences, Widmore Pharmaceuticals, and the Hanso Foundation that funded both the DHARMA Initiative and Paik Industries (owned by Sun's father). The island's original inhabitants – presumably descendants of earlier shipwreck survivors or indigenous peoples – are unaligned with any of these corporations but are nevertheless involved with them.[9] The Hostiles purged the island of the DHARMA Initiative personnel (leaving only Ben who joined them, along with Inman and Rudzinsky who were isolated in the Swan station at the time of the purge), then occupied or made use of their establishments and to some extent took over their operations on the island. Certainly, DHARMA continues to function in some form in the outside world. The supply drops by parachute still take place, so it must be presumed that the Others continue to employ DHARMA personnel off-island and run the finances of the company. As is revealed in 'The New Man in Charge', two operatives at the DHARMA Logistics Warehouse in Guam have continued to prepare and send out palettes loaded with supplies on drones for twenty years.[10] The Others are able to leave and return to the island using the DHARMA Initiative's submarine, although under Ben's leadership those on the island have very little contact with the outside world. The Others have clearly appropriated and taken over the organisation and finances of DHARMA after the purge, though it is never made clear whether or how they also purged any personnel off-island (DHARMA had its headquarters in Ann Arbor and the Lamp Post station in Los Angeles remained operational, although automated). The two warehouse men in 'New Man' have presumably been paid for the time they have been working there, and Ben gives them a substantial severance package suggesting that the Others have access to large sums of money (presumably, DHARMA's). Furthermore, the Others have the resources to make use of front companies to recruit new personnel. Principally this appears to be Mittelos Bioscience, while Herarat Aviation, the company base to which Juliet is directed once she has been recruited, might be another. There is nothing to suggest that any of the images of the Mittelos research facility and personnel that Alpert shows Juliet in 3.7 'Not In Portland' have any basis in reality – 'Well, actually, we're not quite in Portland', Alpert admits during his attempts to recruit her – and the slides he shows her are clearly faked. According to Juliet when she questions Alpert about the need to take the tranquiliser for the journey in 3.16 'One of Us', 'no-one in the medical community has ever heard of Mittelos Bioscience'. Nonetheless, Mittelos also appears (or at least did in the past) to run science camps for gifted teenagers, Locke's teacher having received a brochure from Alpert. Whether or not companies such as Mittelos Biosciences are actual or puppet organisations within the *Lost* universe, they fit within the dominant mode of representations of scientific corporations within the series, that is as research and development organisations exploiting the very nature of the island. Chief amongst the phenomena that the island exhibits are the source of the electromagnetism that the button in the Swan was ostensibly designed to keep in check and the temporal distortions around the island that are revealed in season four.

Corporate control of science and technology has been a significant element of recent science fiction cinema and television. The roles of such corporations in science fiction are not necessarily nefarious but they often shadowy and they may also be linked to military contracts or repressive regimes; examples include the Weyland-Yutani Corporation in *Alien*, Cyberdyne Systems in *The Terminator* (1984), and Massive Dynamic in *Fringe* (2008-13). On Lost, the DHARMA Initiative is established as filling the role of an organisation working to possess and commodify information and technologies. However, DHARMA presents itself, albeit duplicitously, in terms of a rather different scientific discourse, one that is about saving the world rather than controlling it. Nonetheless, DHARMA also represents the imperial coloniser of the island. With their supposedly superior knowledge and equipment they cover the island with research stations, wall themselves inside a fortified compound and regard the 'natives' as 'hostile'. But in doing so they neglect to consider the rights of the colonised, and the 'natives' eventually execute a revolution, taking the island back for themselves.

Control of the island is thus established as a structuring theme in the series. In their discussion of Weyland-Yutani in the *Alien* films, Ximena Gallardo and Jason Smith (2004: 61) argue that the anxieties encoded in science fiction are related to 'self-centred autocracy, corporate technocratic capitalism, sexism, subversion, covert operations and warmongering'. These traits can be identified within the oppositional role that the Widmore Corporation plays in the narrative. After his expulsion from the island, Charles Widmore seeks only to return. The Widmore Corporation is the means by which he can gain his revenge on Ben (ostensibly the CEO of DHARMA). As Miles says to Ben, 'he's put a lot of time and energy into finding you'. Various Widmore enterprises appear to extend their control widely and they have an omnipresence within the series. Indeed, Widmore could be seen as a manipulator of events just as much as Ben or Alpert are: Widmore Construction are working on the Battersea Power Station when Charlie's band Drive Shaft are filming a video; Widmore Labs sponsored Henry Gale's balloon, and made the pregnancy test used by Sun; and the Widmore Corporation organised the boat race that Widmore himself manoeuvered Desmond into participating in. Widmore Corporation is not only a typical shadowy (and possible shady) multinational organisation, but Charles Widmore uses the financial resources at his disposal via the company not only to find the island (he pays £380,000 at an auction in London for a journal from the Black Rock, for example), but to cover up what happened to Oceanic Flight 815 (he acquires 324 dead bodies and a Boeing 777 in order to fake up the wreckage of the plane on the ocean floor). He also organises two expeditions to locate and take back the island (though neither expedition is wholly successful and the second results in his death). Unlike DHARMA, which at least on the surface seeks to prevent or delay the predicted end of the world (a benign aim underscored by their Taoist corporate logo), the Widmore Corporation represents control through status, ownership and power. In *Lost*, the island thus serves as a nexus for the emerging tensions and conflict around corporate culture and autocracy (as well as the issues of femininity, reproduction and technology discussed in chapter 3).

Reflecting this, the arrival of the freighter Kahana on the island signifies the end of cohesion amongst the survivors, a splitting up of the groups and of the timelines. In terms of the unified groupings of survivors and Others, Locke and Juliet are both now associated with the opposite community and sides are redrawn. In 4.1 'The Beginning of the End', Locke's speech at the radio tower signals the setting up of these new sides; he asks the group to go with him to the Others' Barracks since they are the safest place and defendable. 'If you want to live, you have to come with me,' he says, but the location he has chosen not only prefigures his role as one of the Others (if not their leader), but usurps the ruling elite. Ben is the survivors' captive at this point, but aligns himself with Locke: 'Everyone who stays here is going to die,' he tells Danielle. The new group of outsiders from the Kahana are thus configured as the dangerous other to the Others and to the survivors equally (though Jack still looks to them for rescue, leaving the island will not turn out to be a solution to anything).

Furthermore, the freighter carries both a science team and a mercenary unit. Initially, science is not linked here with peace or saving the world, but with conquest and revenge. The allegiances and intentions of the scientists and their allies (Daniel Faraday, Charlotte Lewis, Miles Straume and Frank Lapidus) are ambiguous at the outset, though they are ultimately not seeking the same ends as the military team led by Martin Keamy. This creates a narrative opposition familiar from classic 1950s science fiction cinema, however in *Lost* this opposition is further complicated by the antinomy of science versus faith. Locke, the man of faith rather than the man of science, says to Miles that he is 'responsible for the well-being of this island' (4.4 'Eggtown'). Miles himself is a liminal character linked to science through his father, the DHARMA scientist Pierre Chang – the Marvin Candle of the DHARMA initiation films – and to faith as he can communicate with the dead and worked as a spiritualist before coming to the island. Locke has appointed himself, or believes he has been appointed, the island's protector, but it is Charlotte and Daniel, the scientists, who must shut down the Tempest to prevent the spread of toxic gas that could kill everyone on the island (4.06 'The Other Woman'). It is Daniel in particular who is the key figure in terms of knowledge about the properties of the island.

Unstuck in Time

The proof of the island's unique physical characteristics come with Daniel's arrival on the island; these have simply been part of the mystery and unexplained up to this point. Previously established that the island is a centre of electromagnetic phenomena (the reason for the Swan, the obstetric problems, and possibly the healing properties), his scientific observations now anchor the narrative firmly in science fiction territory. In

4.2 'Confirmed Dead' it is indicated that light is different on the island: 'The light, it's strange out here isn't it?' Daniel notes, 'It's kinda like, it doesn't scatter...quite right.' In 4.3 'The Economist', he arranges for a crew member on the Kahuna to launch a rocket with a clock in the nose cone. On the boat, Regina counts down the decreasing distance of the rocket to Daniel's beacon, but at zero it has not arrived. Daniel finds this 'far more than weird', and some kind of time delay or time distortion between the island and the freighter is apparent (even though radio transmissions are taking place normally). When the rocket finally does arrive, the clock from Daniel's beacon on the island reports the time as 02:45:03, but that from the rocket reads 03:16:22, a thirty-one-minute difference. This notion of 'lost time' connects obliquely to Mittelos, one of the several anagrammatic names used in the series.

Whatever causes the time delay is also clearly a factor in being unable to leave the island. Previously it had been established that travelling there was a difficult process, Juliet and others having to be sedated for the journey. Daniel warns Lapidus to 'be sure that you follow the same exact bearing that we came in on, okay. No matter what. By that, I mean no matter what. Just, just stay on it.' Flying Desmond and Sayid to the freighter, Lapidus knows its location, but can only reach it with the aid of Daniel's instructions. He knows where it is, but *when* it is may be a better question; it is only forty miles off the coast but they take off from the island at dusk and land on the Kahuna in the middle of the day after flying through a thundercloud (4.5 'The Constant'). To Jack and those on the beach the helicopter has been gone for a day, but those on board have not yet arrived at the freighter (a 20-minute journey according to Juliet). Daniel tells them: 'Your perception of how long your friends have been gone? It's not necessarily how long they've actually been gone.'

According to Daniel there are side effects to crossing the time difference between the island and the outside world: 'going to and coming from the island, some people can get a little... confused.' As they fly through the storm, Desmond jumps in time back to his years in the army. When he returns to the helicopter, he is amnesiac. Daniel links these displacements, as he calls them, to Desmond's previous exposure to high levels of electromagnetism when he imploded the Swan. The elements of this plot line (yet another complexity of the neo-baroque narrative) serve as intertexts of the time travel genre. Desmond is not physically travelling in time using some device (as in a series like *Doctor Who*), but his consciousness has become unstuck in time, like Billy Pilgrim in *Slaughterhouse-Five* (1972) or Sam Beckett in *Quantum Leap* (1989-93). This is 'unpredictable', according to Daniel. 'It's a random effect. Sometimes the split takes only a couple of hours, sometimes it's years.' To Desmond, it is from 2004 to 1996. Although physically travelling through time is not possible, knowledge and information can be relayed to the past. Daniel instructs Desmond: 'When it happens again, [...] I need you to get on a train. Get on a train and go to Oxford. Oxford University. Queen's College Physics Department. Alright?' and then:

> When you find me at Queen's College, I need you to tell me to set the device to 2.342. [...] Alright, you got it? 2.342! And it must be oscillating at 11 hertz. [...] And one more thing, Desmond. If the numbers don't convince me, I need you to tell me that you know about Eloise.

This is a relatively complex approach to time travel drama. From Desmond's point of view Daniel relaying this information in the present and his going to see Daniel at Oxford in 1996 are contiguous. One event immediately follows the other in a cause and effect chain despite the second event taking place eight years before. The Daniel of 1996 does not know Desmond because he has not (yet) given him the instructions, so from Daniel's perspective they have never met. In the future, Daniel does not remember having met Desmond, but this is not a paradox. Desmond says that maybe future Daniel had forgotten, which Daniel cannot accept: 'How would that happen?' he says. Yet Daniel might well have forgotten, his experiments – as will be revealed in 5.14 'The Variable' – having scrambled his memory. The numbers that Daniel gave Desmond (in point of fact, they are numbers that Daniel gives himself) will unstick Eloise (the lab rat) in time – 'just like you,' he says to Desmond. In a conflation of temporally disparate moments possible only in science fiction drama, Desmond's meeting with Daniel in 1996 takes place before his conversation with Daniel on the island has concluded, his consciousness returning to the freighter as Keamy is still wrestling the phone from him by force. He had been in the past for at least the time it took to travel from Glasgow to Oxford and find Daniel, though he had been gone only an instant in the present. Similarly, when unconscious in Daniel's lab, Desmond was in 2004 for five minutes, but 'gone' from 1996 for over an hour.

Figure 5: Daniel Faraday fills the role of mad scientist (episode 4.5 The Constant © ABC)

Such time differences between one 'place' and another are common in fantasy fiction such as the Narnia books where the children spend years in the other world but are gone for only minutes from the real one. This scenario on *Lost* is not fantasy, however, and Daniel's role as physicist anchors these tropes in science fiction. As he works at the blackboard scribbling equations, he fulfills the role of the 'mad scientist' character (figure 5). He reveals that Desmond's chance for survival (the lab rat having died of a brain aneurism due to being unable to cope with the time displacement, just as Minkowski does back on the freighter) is to find his anchor, something familiar that he really cares about in both times. Desmond simultaneously rushes to find Penny in 1996 and speak with her from the freighter in 2004. In the language of mathematics, Daniel calls this anchor a constant. Other discourses of this nature reinforce the generic conventions; as well as being surrounded by equations and scientific notations (on his blackboard at Oxford, in his journal), Daniel has studied space time 'all his life', is linked to the Kerr Metric and thus the geometry of spacetime in general relativity, and his death takes place in episode 5.14 'The Variable', the title itself signifying the counterpart to the constant.

Daniel also represents an inversion of the classic 'grandfather paradox' of time travel fiction (this paradox being that if a traveller went back in time and killed his grandfather before he was born, he would never exist to go back in time). Science fiction has sometimes dealt with this through the concept of the multiverse, where the original time line remains and the event that changes time creates not a paradox but a splitting to create a parallel or alternative timeline. However, Daniel argues this is not the case according to the laws of time depicted in the *Lost* universe. He is adamant on several occasions that time cannot be changed. Rather than embodying a grandfather paradox, Daniel goes back in time and is killed by his mother before he is born. He can still be born, and is, of course. No paradox exists, but in an interesting twist on the theme, his date of death is earlier than his date of birth, and his mother is younger when she kills him than she is when she gives birth to him. This becomes not a catastrophe of historical continuity, but a personal tragedy. As Daniel says to Eloise just before he dies: 'You knew, you always knew, but you sent me here anyway.' Eloise must raise her son knowing that she has always already killed him. It is no wonder, then, that she appears so cold and distant to him, why she forces him to become a scientist rather than a musician, why she is insistent he focuses on his work and not his relationship with Theresa, why she informs him he has 'no time for women' (for she knows he will die young), and why she insists he has a 'unique destiny'. A variation of the grandfather paradox of science fiction is the story wherein the time traveller must go back in time and create himself, literally becoming his own father. Constance Penley (1990: 120) discusses this in terms of the primal scene (and the variant of this found in *Terminator*). In *Lost*, however, it is not the traveller who becomes the voyeur at his own conception, but the mother who becomes aware of the presence of her future son as she conceives. Although Daniel's conception is not explicitly depicted in the series, the timeline of *Lost* implies that he may well be born within nine months of his death; Eloise is potentially already pregnant with the man she kills. Penley's account of time travel as primal scene suggests that 'fantasy allows the fact of incest to be both stated and dissimulated' (1990: 122). Daniel is thus intimately linked (through the act of death rather than the act of sex) with his mother at the moment of conception.

It is therefore also noteworthy that Daniel and Charlotte's relationship is experienced as a temporal loop. He develops feelings for her as they randomly move through time after Ben has turned the frozen wheel under the Orchid station. But the temporal displacements cause her death, and just before she dies she tells Daniel of how a scary man came to her when she was a child on the island (her parents worked for DHARMA) and told her never to return to it or she would die (5.5 'This Place is Death'). That scary man is of course Daniel and in 5.8 'LaFleur' he will indeed try and warn her when she is a child in 1974 (where they end up after Locke has turned the wheel again in order to stop the time jumps). Daniel thus attempts to create a paradox, a situation where he will stop her coming to the island, therefore never falling in love with her, and never knowing her to warn her not to return. In other words, he breaks his own rule of time. In Daniel's own theoretical account of time, this is impossible and can only end in failure.

Nonetheless, when other such temporal loops are structured around Desmond they seem to be effective, and furthermore he becomes an increasingly messianic character as the series progresses (and in season six, he will be coded as angelic, directing the survivors into the afterlife). In 'The Constant', Desmond must complete his loop. With the consciousness and knowledge of his future self, he visits Penny in 1996 to tell her to expect his call on Christmas Eve 2004 (his present). His motivation for seeing her is to get her new phone number so that he *can* phone her in 2004 (bringing his constant into the equation and saving his own life). Again, when she tells him the number in 1996, from his perspective it is the same moment that he calls her in 2004. He cannot write the number down, because he can take nothing with him to the future but his memory. When she answers, his memory is restored and he is anchored in time once again.

Quantum physics and space-time thus underpin the various developments in *Lost* from season four onwards as time and time travel become a central trope of the narrative. The previous narrative structure of linear island time inter-cut with flashbacks to characters' lives before the island is disrupted. As the opening scenes of seasons two and three illustrate, the use of an apparent flashback misdirects the viewer. The first shot of papayas against a blue sky in 4.1 'The Beginning of the End' lulls the viewer into thinking the sequence may well be taking place on the island. This is quickly disrupted as a car crashes through the pile of fruit – a signal that this is not the island. Further, this might be interpreted as a flashback. But this reading too is ruptured when the sequence ends with Hurley shouting to the police that he is one of the 'Oceanic 6'. The flashback has now been supplemented by the flashforward, revelations about what will happen to six characters after leaving the island. In terms of the overall narrative structure of the season, they will not escape the island until the final episode (4:14 'There's No Place Like Home part 3'), but their post-island futures are already being recounted from 'The Beginning of the End'. Just like Desmond, the viewer is being positioned into seeing events through time displacement. The sense of place in the *Lost* timeline is flipping between present and future, as well as present and past. This opens up philosophical questions about the nature of existence that are explored in chapter 5.

Chapter 5: The Orchid

The narrative themes of time travel, reproductive technology, and the alien other contextualise *Lost* as science fiction, but the genre is also signified in other ways throughout the series. Of particular relevance is the way science fiction narratives draw on a wide range of cultural intertexts. Specifically, in *Lost* this takes the form of discourses on major strands of philosophical thought. Juneko Robinson makes the point that 'fear, anxiety, dread, passion, death and human finitude, along with the possibility of individual transcendence, freedom and personal responsibility are central concerns not only of horror and many science fiction and fantasy films and literature, but also of much of Western philosophy in general' (2009: 24). There are many potential readings of *Lost* that engage with philosophy (see Kaye 2010, for example), and the range of these illustrate the polysemic nature of the *Lost* narrative. Running throughout *Lost*, as well as through the transmedia story extensions that provided additional narrative material between seasons, many clues were provided as to why the island itself was central to the lives of so many groups of people. Characters felt a strong connection to the island, felt there was a reason they had been brought to the island, felt that it had given them a purpose or new outlook on life, and were deeply affected on a physical, emotional or spiritual level. Questions of fate, destiny and free will were thus revisited again and again, but moreover, the science fiction tropes employed by the series linked strongly to the opposition of social control versus freedom.

Michael Rennett argues that the very narrative structure of *Lost* with its flashbacks, flashforwards, flash-sideways and time travel means that the story 'mirrors the programme's philosophical debate between fate and free will' (2011: 26). The different timelines and the way in which these timelines intersect and overlap is part of the larger puzzle of *Lost* for the cult audience, and for Rennett this means that viewers 'can find a thrill in witnessing the unintentional off-island encounters between the Oceanic survivors before the crash since it adds to the show's philosophical ambiguity' (2011: 27). Coincidence or fate is the key narrative opposition here, and Rennett's schema of different manipulations of temporal flow fit within the series as time travel drama. Determinist and fatalist flashbacks are integral to the narrative, and furthermore the flashforwards maintain the sense of predestination in the narrative by presenting the future as inevitable and inexorable (Rennett 2011: 33). More importantly, actual movements across time when the characters are subjected to random and uncontrollable time jumps in season five, clearly establish the fact – and Daniel Faraday gives repeated reminders of this – that they are unable to change the future. And should they try, they will merely be providing the set of circumstances that they have always already experienced in their present (the future from their point of view in the past). The timeline is fixed and unchangeable.

Actions and events are not only preordained, but characters must perform certain acts in a certain order in order to fulfill their destiny. They have no choice, and no opportunity to change the outcome or alter the timeline. This supposes that there is no choice in the matter: Desmond must go to the island, Daniel must be shot by Eloise, Kate and Sawyer must take Ben to Alpert. Desmond must save Charlie several times because Charlie must go to the Looking Glass (where he is destined to die). All of them must get on the plane, and in fact as the series develops many of the flashbacks are employed in the service of setting out the efforts required to get them to the airport and onto that flight on time. Even when the Oceanic 6 have escaped and gone back to their lives, they come to accept that they must return to the island. Nevertheless, on the micro-level of their everyday lives characters still assert their right to free will. Juliet still asserts her right to freely choose a book that Ben does not like, just as Daniel still attempts to stop Charlotte returning to the island even though he is the one asserting that history cannot be changed. The narrative tropes of the time travel drama also suggest one particular reading of the flash-sideways in season six, that the explosion of the bomb created an alternate timeline (where the island is sunk beneath the waves and where flight 815 lands safely at LAX). This multiverse interpretation is one that chimes with science fiction fans, and with those viewers with some understanding of quantum mechanics. However, the narrative framing of the alternative parallel world in *Lost* is very different from those depicted in *Fringe*, *Counterpart* (2017-19) or *The Man in the High Castle* (2015-19). The fact that the final episode of *Lost* reveals the nature of the flash-sideways as metaphysical (it is a purgatory in which the characters must achieve a degree of enlightenment before 'moving on') demands another approach to the science fiction tropes used in the series.

Science fiction frequently encompasses religion, science, and philosophy within its narrative at both a textual and a subtextual level; it is frequently engaged with the metaphysical as well as the physical universe. As Susan Schneider proposes, 'Philosophy and science fiction are converging upon a set of shared themes and questions' (2009: 2). The genre thus engages with questions of free will, of identity and what it is to be conscious, what it means to be human, the nature of space and time, and whether reality really is what we think it is. According to John Taylor, 'science fiction provides a genre in which metaphysical questions concerning the ultimate structure of reality regularly arise' (2003: 20). Introduced in the fifth season of *Lost*, the Orchid station is built above what DHARMA scientists describe as a 'pocket of [...] negatively charged exotic matter' (as Pierre Chang explains on the orientation film shown in 4.13 'There's No Place Like Home part 2') and houses the frozen wheel which Ben turns to move the island. On one level, the Orchid was the base for space-time experiments involving the transportation of rabbits through time. This fits neatly with the time travel themes introduced during season four, but rather than suggesting a straightforward time travel narrative, however, *Lost* uses generic conventions such as these to question the nature of reality. In this case, how can an island move? How can the person who turns the wheel suddenly arrive in Tunisia? Answers (at least according to the conventions of science fiction) are not forthcoming. They remain part of a complex web of philosophical and metaphysical allusions within the series.

Being and being named

Further to Rennett's point about temporal flow being linked to these strains of philosophical thought, the characters themselves suggest important elements in the themes of the series. Moreover, the naming of characters is a significant component of these generic themes. Names have long been employed as part of a generic repertoire; as Fowler (1982) argues, characters' names are indicators of their links to particular genres and can also signal shifts from one genre to another. Character names have great significance in *Lost*, and in particular they are used as signifiers of philosophical themes. These meanings both relate to the roles the characters play and push the narrative meaning in particular directions. Names are not only used to define character, give clues to personality, and suggest narrative placement, but they are 'names that gesture outward from the series' (Gilbert 2005). The character names connote themes that are external to the plot and suggest meanings that extend beyond the obvious causation patterns and character motivations of the narrative. They thus provided discursive patterns; they are positioned outside of the unified spatio-temporal order of the narrative but they nevertheless produce narrative knowledge. Names, then, are second order story elements that make sense within the logic of the narrative, but are positioned between plot and explanation. According to Sarah Worth, 'the discursive mode relies on logical, linear reasoning' (2004: np), and drawing on the work of narrative psychologist Jerome Bruner, she asserts that such discursive elements establish a formal truth, as opposed to the generic verisimilitude of the narrative. Worth draws on the examples of the Sherlock Holmes stories and Edgar Allen Poe's detective fiction to illustrate her point. These kinds of text are presented in the form of a narrative, but the narrative aspects of the fiction are positioned alongside the discursive clues that the reader has to follow in order to work out the mystery:

> The discursive mode allows us to see logical connections between states of affairs prior to being able to prove them empirically. It further allows us the faculty of abstract reasoning, which can go above and beyond the particular example of any given situation. [...] The narrative mode, in opposition to the discursive, will lead to good stories, and believable dramatic and historical accounts. The narrative mode looks primarily for human (and not necessarily or exclusively logical) connections between characters and events. (Worth 2004: np)

A similar relationship between the discursive and the narrative modes can be identified in *Lost*, and whilst the naming of characters is not the only element of this, it is a significant one.

Naming falls into the three main interconnected categories that relate to the generic themes: the religious, the scientific and the philosophical. The scientific naming, for example, makes direct link to the themes of science and technology present in the series and the wider generic tropes of science fiction. Michael Faraday, the natural philosopher, is known for his work in electromagnetic fields, but most notably he posited a link between magnetism and light, establishing that a magnetic force could affect the polarisation of light (known as the Faraday effect). One of Daniel Faraday's first remarks on the island is that the light is strange because it doesn't scatter normally (4.2 'Confirmed Dead'). He observes the Faraday effect. In effect, the original Faraday is present and commenting on the island's properties through *Lost*'s own Faraday. Similarly, the names Eloise Hawking (after Stephen Hawking, the cosmologist most well-known for *A Brief History of Time*) and Kelvin Inman (after the temperature scale developed by Lord Kelvin) carry connotations of space-time and thermodynamics respectively.

It is the metaphysical naming in *Lost* that is the more interesting, though, in relation to the antinomies of order and chaos, fate and chance, and science and faith. The religious and the philosophical are the key areas in this respect, and several of the major character names contribute to narrative knowledge. Many Judeo-Christian names are used in the series: James (Sawyer) is one of the disciples, as is his brother John (Locke); Aaron (Claire's son) and Daniel (Faraday) are significant figures from the Hebrew scriptures; both parts of Christian Shephard's name refer to Jesus, as the Christ and as the shepherd of men (though this is in contradiction with his actions which seem very un-Christ-like). Other religions are also referenced in this signification process. Dharma stands out, related as it is to Buddhist teachings and law, and to the Sanskrit word meaning 'natural law' or 'cosmic order'. It refers both to an ultimate reality and to the path that one must follow in order to achieve enlightenment. The DHARMA symbol (its brand identity) reflects the I Ching symbology, the Taoist method of divination. This connection with Eastern religion and philosophy is written into the narrativity of the series; the Hindi salutation 'namaste' being used by the DHARMA Initiative personnel when they welcome new recruits to the island, shown on a sign in the Barracks and used by Chang in the orientation films.

More importantly in terms of key narrative knowledge, though, are Benjamin and Jacob. The Biblical Benjamin is the son of Jacob, and a logical connection can be drawn to his namesake Ben Linus. On *Lost*, Ben is the direct subordinate of Jacob;

he claims that only he can make contact and communicate with the unseen 'father'. According to the account in Genesis, Benjamin was the youngest son of Jacob and his mother died shortly after giving birth to him. Ben's mother too dies in childbirth; both women name their son just before they die (Genesis 35: 16-18 and 3:20 'The Man Behind the Curtain'). The circumstances of Ben's birth are also the reason for his being on the island, the man who helped his parents on the day of his birth being Horace Goodspeed, a mathemetician and leader of the DHARMA group on the island, who gets Ben's father a position with DHARMA. The name 'Goodspeed' is itself a modern version of the Medieval surname Godspede meaning 'may God speed you', a goodwill courtesy offered to those setting out on a journey. Although not directly related to the story of Jacob and Benjamin, Goodspeed is the builder of the cabin in which Jacob is said to reside by Ben (although when Locke and Hurley are there it appears to be the Man in Black who is occupying it). Goodspeed appears in a dream to Locke, directing him to find his body in the mass grave, the plans and location for the cabin being in the pocket of his jumpsuit (4.11 'Cabin Fever').

Furthermore, in Genesis, Jacob and his twin brother Esau, the sons of Isaac, are described as being at war with each other. They struggled while still in the womb (Genesis 25: 22-23) and it was prophesied that they would be divided with the older (Esau) serving the younger (Jacob). Jacob on *Lost* also has a brother who, while not sharing the name, is coded as the 'bad twin' (he is always dressed in dark clothing while Jacob is always in light-coloured clothing) and logically therefore Esau – though in the series Jacob is the elder twin. There is also a flash frame in the room 23 video used by DHARMA to wipe the memories of Hostiles they have captured (and which the Hostiles later use on Walt and Karl, and which Jin sees when held by Widmore's people) which states: 'God loves you as he loved Jacob.' Narratively, the Jacob of the Bible can be connected to the Jacob of the island, and *Lost* can be read as a contemporary reworking of the Biblical story in order to address the anxieties of the age, including inequality, conflict, and destruction. Jacob first kills and is then killed by his brother, he and the Man in Black constantly enact and re-enact the same battle. This is the endless warfare of the modern world.

Given that names are so significant, there must be equal significance in the fact that Jacob's twin has no name. 'I only picked one name,' his mother Claudia says before the woman referred to only as Mother kills her. On the one hand, this depersonalises them. The characters become signifiers of their own roles – the Great Matriarch (she is figuratively positioned as the transcendent and cosmic Virgin-Mother), and the man with no name (the Man in Black is literally encoded as the evil man). When Jack and Locke find their skeletons in the caves, not knowing they are (adoptive) mother and son, they refer to them as Adam and Eve, the universal parents. On the other hand, being unnamed conveys status and power. In China, for example, the Emperor's name was seen to hold such power that it was forbidden to speak it, and in Judaism it is forbidden to utter the true name of God. It is also noteworthy that in certain folk tales characters have a need to keep their names secret; knowledge of a supernatural helper or evil entity's real name in folktales vanquishes them, as in Rumpelstilzchen, Whuppity Stoorie, and Tom-Tit-Tot. In terms of the discursive mode, there are clear narrative reasons for the Man in Black and Mother to go unnamed.

As Jack David Zipes states: 'To name is to know, to recognise, to become secure through knowledge so that one can protect oneself' (1994: 51). In *Lost*, the Man in Black seemingly has no true name to learn, and this empowerment and security is encoded into the narrative through the difficulties of identifying him. His appearance as Locke (variously referred to by fans and in the media as Fake Locke/Flock, Smock and Un-Locke in an attempt to name the entity) means that various characters have to un-recognise Locke and realise that 'he' is the Man in Black/smoke monster. Similarly, Dogen seeks to determine whether the resurrected Sayid is 'infected' by torturing him with electric shocks and hot pokers: a figurative recognition of his true name or nature (Sayid fails this test and later aids Fake Locke by murdering Lennon and Dogen – in this case they may have learnt his 'true name' but it did not empower them). It has also been suggested by Géza Róheim and Alan Dundes (1992: 126) that this type of story is a dream narrative, the speaking of the true name standing in for the moment of awakening from the nightmare.[11] It can therefore be seen as significant that Jacob and the Man in Black's life stories – and thus identities – are only revealed at the very end of the series (6.15 'Across the Sea') just as the characters in the flash-sideways 'wake up' to the nature of their existence in purgatory. The nature of reality and free will are in this way linked to notions of control and being manipulated by a higher power.

Being and Being Seen

In terms of control, the Swan station, the Barracks and the Hydra island all open up the theme of security, surveillance and imprisonment, as does the Lighthouse. The science fiction genre often reflects social and political anxieties circulating in contemporary culture through its representation of the control that science and technology exert over the lives of the characters. In *Lost*, such examples of control take two principle forms: the first being the way in which technology is used to control individuals and groups, and the second, the ways in which the island itself impacts upon the lives of the occupants. The links here are frequently made through the philosophical themes alluded to by *Lost*'s character names, primarily John Locke, Desmond Hume and Danielle Rousseau.[12] One of David Hume's key philosophical arguments concerns human nature and the concept of identity, with Hume arguing that beliefs in the fixed and unchanging reality of the self and the existence of the external world cannot be justified. Hume concluded that scepticism is the only defensible view of the world, and also that passion rather than reason dictates actions. Desmond Hume neatly fits this model: his careers, if not his identity, are shifting (he is seen in various 'jobs' – a monk, a soldier and a round the world yachtsman, and he tells Jack that he was a set designer and might have been a doctor), his timeline is not fixed (he can 'see' the future after the Swan implodes, his consciousness shifts between his time in the army and being on the freighter, and he becomes unstuck in time going back to visit Faraday during his years at Oxford), he seems more of a sceptic than a man of faith (despite what he says to Jack about miracles and his attempts to become a monk, his old girlfriend tells him that the nearest thing he has had to a religious experience is when Celtic won the cup), and he acts out of passion not reason (his love for Penny, his abandonment of her, his decision to take Widmore's challenge). It is also worth noting that Hume the philosopher was linked to Jean-Jacques Rousseau. Desmond and Danielle are both loners on the island, not part of any of the other groupings and communities, and therefore represent independence and individuality. Rousseau argued that mankind is essentially good and can achieve the natural condition of the 'noble savage' when living in the 'state of nature' – just as Danielle seems to. Though in his later work, Rousseau backtracked by arguing that good men only arise within societies, here too parallels can be seen in Danielle and her 'successor' Claire having lost the civilizing influence of society. They are both depicted as wild (or in a brutish condition according to Rousseau's writings): living alone, alienated and paranoid, their hair unruly and in disarray, a rifle constantly at hand, and singularly distrustful and lacking empathy. Rousseau was also regarded as eccentric, arrogant and having a martyr complex – all of which could be applied to Danielle, especially in relation to the loss of her daughter. It is worth noting that in terms of the Swan and Locke's role on the island, the numbers have a socializing influence, rendering the equally individualised Locke a part of the hegemonic system.

More importantly, John Locke is a key figure in the construction of narrative knowledge. The original Locke's philosophical writings are concerned with opposition to authoritarianism; similarly, *Lost*'s Locke continually objects to being told what he can't do. This becomes a repeated motif throughout the series: in 1.4 'Walkabout' he says it to his boss at the box company, to the travel agent who denies him a place on the walkabout, and to Kate on the island. Similarly, in 1.19 'Deus Ex Machina', he says it to Boone (the only member of the community he is closely associated with and his apprentice of sorts) when he refuses to accept the impossibility of opening the hatch. In addition, it is (at least initially) linked to his disability. To his boss he cites the example of a double amputee who climbed Everest and to the travel agent he claims a destiny. Whether or not he refuses to accept his limitations, both these examples are cases where he rejects the views of those who have authority or control over him. This establishes him as someone who wants to choose his own path and fight against those who stand in his way, he is not signified as meek or subservient in any way. His confrontation with Kate over the futility of hunting boar also encodes him as an individualist. Although he is working for the group in obtaining food, he does not seem concerned for a fellow survivor's health and wellbeing. Where Kate's concerns are for the injured Michael, Locke's refusal to give up the hunt signifies him as someone who positions himself outside of the community, a loner. Furthermore, this stance is revealed as being unrelated to his disability and it is suggested that he has been in a lifelong battle with authority. In a flashback to his childhood in 'Cabin Fever', he says it to his teacher in response to being advised that he is the man of science not the man of action. Locke's philosophical stance on the island suggests he wishes to accord free will and choice to everyone; in 2.11 'The Hunting Party' he asks the rhetorical question: 'Who are we to tell anyone what they can or can't do?' When Locke breaks his own code and attempts to control others, they turn his words back on him (Charlie in 3.3 'Further Instructions' and Ben in 3.19 'The Brig'). On a figurative level, they have taken his philosophy to heart.

Figure 6: Jack comes under observation from The Pearl surveillance station (episode 2.21 ? © ABC)

After he had turned the wheel under the Orchid and returned to the outside world, Locke was also provided with the alias of another philosopher, Jeremy Bentham (by Charles Widmore in 5.7 'The Life and Death of Jeremy Bentham' – having been assumed dead he cannot go by the name John Locke off the island). Bentham the philosopher was an advocate of utilitarianism, according to which actions that produce greater amounts of happiness (defined as pleasure without pain) are determined as having higher worth. This reflects Locke's embrace of the life on the island: it serves his sense of utilitarianism to believe the island summoned them for a greater purpose (1.24 'Exodus part 2'). His purpose is thus to hunt boar to feed the camp, to become the hunter he has always wanted to be rather than a farmer (3.3 'Further Instructions'). He takes pleasure in opening the hatch not in the hope that it can become a refuge and a hiding place from the Others, but because it offers him a purpose. He pushes the button to prevent disaster, believing that to be its function. This is thrown into question when Locke and Eko locate the Pearl observation station (2.21 '?') and see Jack in the Swan on a video monitor (figure 6). Apparently, entering the numbers is part of a psychological experiment. Though it is later suggested that the psychological experiment may have been conducted on the subjects in the Pearl doing the watching, rather than those in the Swan being watched, the fact of the Pearl being a surveillance operation is crucial to this reading of the series. This central viewing station (it is located in the very centre of the blast door map) brings to mind the philosopher Bentham's concept of the Panopticon. Specifically, the Panopticon is a prison designed around a circular chamber in such a way that every prisoner is under observation by his jailers. Although neither jailer nor prisoner are roles that Locke takes on permanently, he nevertheless displays characteristics of each. Like the other inhabitants of the island he is trapped there, he is the primary 'prisoner' of the Swan station and thus the subject of the apparent psychological experiment being observed from the Pearl. After death, he is the principle human form taken on by the smoke monster – he 'becomes' the Man in Black, the island's and Jacob's prisoner. However, he is also connected intimately with the island itself (which significantly also contains the Lighthouse which was used to observe the candidates in their previous lives), and as the form taken by the black smoke is also a jailer of sorts, or at least a guard. He is also the literal jailer of Ben (on two occasions) and Miles. Locke is thus both prisoner and jailer, observed and observer, in the island as Panopticon. For viewers, already in the position of voyeur, these second order story elements do not directly contribute to plot, but they do create narrative knowledge that can be carried across the series as a whole. This can be part of the game of *Lost* for the fan, and recognition of the source for each character's name can provide additional pleasures from being in the know – a form of cultural capital as defined by Sarah Thornton (1995: 11-12). Fans can carry this over into their engagement with the transmedia storytelling components of *Lost* discussed in the final chapter.

Chapter 6: The Temple

It is in terms of transmedia storytelling where *Lost* stands out as a milestone science fiction series exploiting online and fan culture. Its use of narrative structure and semio-narratological codes to form a puzzle extends into paratexts that work to deepen narrative knowledge, if not narrative development itself. As Marc Dolan says: 'Never in the history of Western civilisation has corporate synergy worked to greater aesthetic effect' (2010: 156). This is important when considering the *Lost* narrative as a game being played with the viewer. Primarily, transmedia storytelling extends the narrative beyond the episodes made for television; commonly this is in the form of short episodes or other media available online. Jason Mittell terms this 'centrifugal storytelling' that takes an 'expansionist approach' to the 'transmedial sphere' (2014: 264). In one respect, this serves the marketing purpose of maintaining a high media profile for the series, keeping the viewer interested between seasons, and providing a hook into each new season.

Telefantasy and science fiction series offer many opportunities for transmedia storytelling with their complex storyworlds, multiple timelines, hyperdiegesis and perpetuated hermeutic, and polysemic narrative knowledge. As Colin Harvey points out, 'the genres of science fiction and fantasy [...] have become the dominant mode of transmedia storytelling' (2015: 1) due, as Paolo Bertetti argues, to the fact that the creation of detailed settings is a 'structural necessity' in these genres 'from a semiotic and narratological point of view' (2017: 47). For viewers, paratexts create alternative ways to find out more about what is going on in *Lost* and to add to their knowledge of the diegetic world depicted in the series. In particular, the fascination with the meaning of the numbers, better access to the maps and other props shown in the series, and curiosity about the people, places and organisations in the *Lost* universe have drawn many viewers into the transmedia texts of *Lost*. Intense fans might also have to work to both find and incorporate this extra-textual material into the storyline. Henry Jenkins defines transmedia storytelling as 'a new aesthetic that has emerged in response to media convergence – one that places new demands on consumers and depends on active participation of knowledge communities' (2006: 20-21). Jenkins equates such participants to hunter-gatherers having to chase down snippets of story across multiple delivery channels and comparing notes with each other in online discussion. As Jenkins states, those who 'invest time and effort will come away with a richer entertainment experience' (2006: 21). Moreover, this serves to create a more detailed and multi-layered hyperdiegetic world (the reason Jenkins refers to transmedia storytelling as 'the art of world making').

The *Lost* viewer is able to find such information in the mobisodes and webisodes referred to in the introduction (the *Lost: Missing Pieces*), for example, as well as various interactive online gaming and video games, the *Lost* novels, and other merchandise. These work to construct a transmedia narrative, and make *Lost* a prime example of what Jenkins (2006) calls convergence culture, or what Christy Dena (2008) perhaps more accurately refers to as integration culture. Regardless of what it is called, however, transmedia storytelling has benefits for the culture industries, creative personnel and audiences alike. Marc Dolan not only describes *Lost* as 'one of the most creative programmes in the history of regularly scheduled broadcast television', but also as 'an organic product of the American entertainment industry' (2010: 149). With the Internet now a key element of the media landscape, its functions and uses are crucial to the culture industries in an integration culture. As Dolan goes on to point out, *Lost* can be seen not as a television series so much as 'more precisely [a] transmedia product of a very large twenty-first-century corporation, a product in process whose shape is nevertheless determined more by its creators and fans than by the corporation that mediates between them' (2010: 156). Moreover, whilst *Lost* viewers can comprehend and enjoy the series well enough from the television episodes alone, the narrative cannot be said to have a single source (an ur-text in Jenkins' account) that provides all of the information needed for fans to completely immerse themselves in the narrative knowledge and universe of *Lost*.

Transmedia *Lost*

As illustrated by *Lost: Missing Pieces*, the maps hidden on the backs of the jigsaw puzzles, and 'The New Man in Charge' coda to the series (discussed in previous chapters), the storylines and hermeneutic codes of *Lost* frequently flow over into the paratexts associated with the series. Jennifer Gillan frames this in terms of her discussion of 'must-click tv', playing on the notion of must-see quality television as practiced in the Internet age, pointing out that 'the web is central to the on-air success of *Lost*' (2011: 155). Ivan Askwith and Jonathan Gray (2008: 525) include amongst the 'innovative and compelling transmedia extensions' of *Lost*: the Oceanic Airlines website that contained clues for solving the mysteries in the series; the *Bad Twin* novel found in the luggage of the crashed plane which was then published as a tie-in novel that could be 'scavenged for narrative clues'; the *Lost Diaries* home video mobisodes; and the alternate reality games. The ARGs represent one of the most significant developments in transmediality, creating, as Elizabeth Evans argues, an 'integrated, coherent narrative experience' (2011: 85). Immersion in the interactive gaming experience can be a significant pleasure for viewers, offering different forms of engagement with the storyworld.

Figure 7: Apollo candy bars produced for The Lost Experience *ARG (© ABC)*

The ARGs that interlinked with *Lost* – *The Lost Experience* between seasons two and three in 2006, *Find 815* in the season four hiatus in 2008, the *DHARMA Initiative Recruiting Project* in the gap between seasons four and five in 2008, and the *Lost University* between seasons five and six in 2009 – are important examples of transmedia storytelling in the service of the culture industries and their new media marketing techniques. In their discussion of transmedia storytelling and media franchises, Askwith and Gray refer to *The Lost Experience* as a 'summer-long interactive narrative *campaign*' (2008: 522, my italics). Hi-ReS!, the design consultancy which produced marketing material for *The Lost Experience*, describe it in their portfolio as a 'multi-media marketing alternate reality game' and refer to it, again as a 'marketing campaign'.[13] *The Lost Experience* veered across press and television advertisements for the Hanso Foundation, a 'fake' Hanso website, the vlog of new character Rachel Blake investigating Hanso, the podcasts made by another new character DJ Dan, Apollo bar giveaways (figure 7), and live character appearances at ComicCon. As Hi-ReS! summarise it, the game 'was designed to unite *Lost* fans from around the world' and:

> [R]evealed the 'back-story' of the Hanso Foundation, the shadowy organisation behind the fictitious Dharma Initiative which sits at the heart of the TV series. A detailed combination of TV adverts, fake websites, call-centres, blogs, chocolate bars, video and flash mobs were co-ordinated to enable users to follow the story of Rachel Blake, an ex-employee of the Hanso Foundation trying to uncover the truth behind the company's sinister activities.

Clearly, there was narrative information within the game, but the foregrounding of sponsor's products – including Verizon, Sprite, Jeep and Monster.com – was rife. The word 'Sprite' occurred more frequently in the game dialogue than the word 'Dharma', for example, and product placement was prominent throughout the game. As Gillan argues, the ARGs are 'less about creative form [...] than they are about creative marketing' (2011: 165). However, this does not take into account the fans' responses to the text (including the ARGs) and the ways in which they use and interpret the semio-narratological codes of the text to inform narrative knowledge and fan competencies.

Despite the fact that the product placement and creative marketing suggests the game was primarily driven by hybrid promotion and commercial practice (Gillan 2011, 165-167), it was still popular with fans dedicated and competent enough to follow the clues, analyse the evidence and discuss within the online *Lost* fan community. Matt Hills's point that fan culture is both distanced from commodification and yet bound up within it is important here. This 'suspensionist' position can accommodate a both/and position in which fans can be 'simultaneously inside and outside processes of commodification' (Hills 2004: 44). The tension between creative form and creative marketing is not one that can be easily reconciled in either direction as the actual consumption and use of the ARGs attests. *The Lost Experience* required a skill set that included understanding source code for web pages and the use of steganography to hide text in digitised images, knowledge of cryptology, hexadecimal, binary and base64 numbering systems, and of classical mythology, and fluency in Korean and Danish (or access to translations), as well as geographical proximity to real-world locations where clues could be found. The point here is that no one person could solve the clues and complete the game alone, but that it could only be achieved by sharing and working together as a group. For example, when Apollo bars with a website address embossed in the chocolate were handed out in comic and sci-fi bookshops, those present could instantaneously share that address with players in other locations. In this way, both the product placement and the narrative elements take a secondary status to sociability and community within the fan culture. Furthermore, viewers did not even have to take part in the game itself to gain knowledge of the narrative elements. Key parts of the game – for example, the video blogs and screen grabs of the websites (which in any case were very often ephemeral) – were quickly made available on YouTube and fan sites.

This often severed (or at least loosened) the connection between the promotional material and the narrative content; the viewers consuming such textual material no longer had to 'exchange attention to advertising in return for entertainment content' as Gillan puts it (2011: 165). For example, content from the *Find 815* ARG was uploaded as narrative scenes (*Find 815 chapter 1*, for example, shows the scene setting up the character Sam Thomas, an Oceanic IT Technician who was engaged to one of the flight attendants on board Oceanic 815), the main clues (such as the hacked Oceanic advert that directs the player towards Sam Thomas's blog), and solutions to the interactive puzzles and other game elements (the circuit board minigame walkthrough, for instance).[14] Although this material is initially provided for other game players and does not replicate the interactive and immersive experience of taking part in the game itself, it does enable the wider distribution of the transmedia story material and allows the non-playing viewer to acquire the additional competencies and knowledge of the larger narrative of *Lost*. This allows access to narrative material about the Sundara Trench where the fake wreckage was located, the role of the Maxwell Group (a division of Widmore Industries), and links to the series such as the scene where Frank Lapidus phones the Oceanic hotline after seeing the footage on television and realising that the man identified as the pilot in the wreckage is not the pilot who flew the actual flight (4.02 'Confirmed Dead').

Although, as Askwith and Grey propose, these ARGs serve a range of creative, promotional and financial purposes, they also form 'synergistic storytelling innovations' as a contrast to 'corporate synergy' (2008: 525). As with the ARGs, various forms of merchandising also serve commerce, but beyond that promise secrets and clues that add to the semio-narratological meanings of the series for fans. As Askwith and Grey note, the *Lost* jigsaws have 'no place in *Lost*'s larger narrative' and provide no additional information; rather they 'take advantage of the show's mysteries, and sell otherwise unremarkable merchandise by "bundling" it with exclusive "insights"' (2008: 525-526). Clearly, fans could study the map from the episode itself using screengrabs, but this also fails to take note of the processes of fan consumption, whereby the fans' uses of the text make it real (Jenkins 1992: 51-53). Accordingly, the fans make use of the episode itself, the jigsaws and the copy of the map in *TV Guide* (as well as the additional layer of the map seen in the video game) to create their own fan texts such as the annotated blast door map with translation legend.[15]

The significance of *Lost* in this respect is that whilst 'concerns regarding the hidden persuasions of product placement and the monopolistic tendencies of synergy continue to exist', they – and *Lost* is a primary example in this – are 'now being accompanied by some writers' and consumers' excitement at the prospect of yet more developed story worlds' (Askwith and Grey 2008: 526). While *Lost* as a traditional media text is clearly not interactive, it offers a semblance of interactivity through its presence on the Internet, on mobile telephony networks and in video games that bring transmedia storytelling to the fore. Such elaborate transmedia campaigns are now commonplace, and *Lost* was an important groundbreaking series in this respect.

Hypertextual *Lost*

The transmedia storytelling, in combination with the non-linear structure and neo-baroque aesthetic, works to create a narrative that resembles a hypertext. As Dolan recognises, at the start of the series 'neither the audience nor the actors know for sure what is true about the characters' lives before they crashed on the island until they see it in flashback' (2010: 152). Personal histories are revealed only slowly and in fragments. This keeps the narrative open, ambiguous and mysterious. Dolan notes that 'the creators meant the show to be like a video game, with additional levels unlocked the longer and more successfully we play' (2010: 153), and as the narrative unfolded new levels in the form of the Swan, the Barracks, the Hydra island, and so on were introduced. New narrative timelines are also opened up with each new level unlocked. Season one has a linear narrative flow with linear sets of flashbacks in each episode relating to each character in turn (one per episode means that it is easy for viewers to make sense of and interpret each story). There are a few hints of connections between characters prior to the plane crash but these are fairly minimal and suggest questions in the viewer's mind without causing major shifts in meaning. In season two, these connections become much stronger, it is suggested that these seemingly random castaways – connected only by a chance booking on the same flight – might actually have been caught in a web of some unknown design or fate much earlier. During season two, replays of time from other points of view also occur, unlocking new story elements and characters. Principally, we see the 'tailies' experience of the first 48 days on the island that had unfolded for the primary set of characters during season one. Similarly, there is a looping back to events of season one to fill in what happened when Ethan kidnapped Claire, and what happened when Michael went off alone to search for Walt. Further, with the introduction of Desmond (previously seen only briefly in Jack's season one flashbacks) moments of island time prior to the crash are opened up, Desmond's arrival on the island and life in the Swan are revealed, as well as the event that caused the plane crash. The flashbacks in later seasons also go further back in time, and not necessarily linearly, as when Locke's attempt to go on walkabout is shown before Widmore's agent Matthew Abbadon urges him to go on such an adventure.

Since the early 1990s, the ways in which television programmes are marketed, transmitted, viewed and talked about has advanced markedly. As Robin Nelson points out, 'Many aspects of television production and reception, as well as our understanding of these processes, have changed' (1997: 1). Even leaving aside the role of the Internet in the expansion of the television landscape for a moment, the technological, economic, institutional, cultural and aesthetic factors of television have been reformulated. This new ecology of television, as Nelson refers to it (1997: 2), is one that *Lost* fully inhabits. It is the kind of drama that offers added-value in these changing circumstances and is a prime example of the increased productivity in meanings and pleasures that television drama can now offer. This acknowledges that one of the most significant changes in television production has been the increasing complexity of narratives. Nelson refers to the multi-narrative, multi-character dramas now commonplace in American television drama as flexi-narratives (1997: 24), but in many ways these are similar to the narrative traits of telefantasy and the neo-baroque aesthetic. *Lost* is an important example of these changes, having the dense textures and multiple perspectives he identifies as key traits of the flexi-narrative. In many respects, these traits, and the concept of the flexi-narrative itself, are linked with the notion of quality television, with series such as *Twin Peaks* representing what Nelson (1997: 12) calls the new paradigm of television drama. In considering this as 'a new way of dealing with a media-saturated, information overload in place of more explanatory sense-making in terms of the linearity of cause and effect in specific contexts' (Nelson 1997: 17), the whole has perhaps less significance than the fragmentary parts. Temporal flow and continuity, disrupted as they are in *Lost* within the episodic narrative and across the range of transmedia texts, has less importance as a structuring device. An example of this is found in Dolan's reading of the flashbacks. Arguing that past and future are equally as palpable as the present, he defines this as 'narratological instability' (2010: 154). The flashbacks represent a coming unstuck in time from the point of view of the characters' own conscious awareness.

Extrapolating from this it is possible to envisage *Lost* as a hypertext, with the flashbacks and flash-forwards, replaying of events from different points of view, and flash-sideways into some form of 'afterlife' representing the televisual equivalents of the 'click-through'. Much more weight is thus given to what Nelson describes as 'the aestheticisation of the image' (1997: 24-5). The image is frequently dominant in *Lost*: in the musical montage sequences that end episodes; in the emphasis on maps and games when depicting the island itself; in the allusions to science, religion and philosophy in the naming of characters; and in the juxtapositions of visually and discursively different time periods and locations. This resembles what Nelson refers to as parataxis – a 'collage of discourses eschewing any attempt to smooth out their differences into a sense-making harmonious whole' (1997: 16). *Lost*, loosely constructed on such a paratactical framework, affords space for readers to actively construct meanings and pleasures – or 'plural cognitions' as Nelson calls them (1997: 28). Undoubtedly, this active construction of meaning and pleasure includes the way the series resembles a jigsaw puzzle that the viewer has to construct for themselves, taking in a range of transmedia texts as well as the television narrative itself.

This is not only the 'unique selling point' of *Lost*, but also its pitfall. In many respects the perpetuated hermeneutic and neo-baroque aesthetic were too complex for casual viewers who, lacking the dedication and intense scrutiny of the telefantasy fan, became (literally) lost in the hypertext. *Lost* demands concentrated viewing and this benefits from the transmedia storytelling but at the same time excludes casual viewers. There are similarities here to Nelson's account of *Twin Peaks*: 'It may well be that the decentring tendencies of *Twin Peaks*, its refusal to accommodate the desire for followability or to allow comfortable viewing positions are precisely those features which a regular audience rejects' (1997: 239). Undoubtedly, viewers who find *Lost* difficult might well lose interest, but on the other hand the fact that a series like *Lost* is not 'easy watching' contributes to its cult status. The flexi-narrative form and the long arc-story of cult television have led to longer duration narratives (with plotlines ongoing across as well as within seasons), and *Lost* has one of the most complex long-arc storylines of contemporary television. The processes of production and reception continued to change as the technologies of the Internet and online connectivity rapidly evolved across the time period of *Lost*'s six seasons. Production and reception both adapted to take account not only of the episodes of the television series itself, but a wide and varied range of associated material. *Lost* was ideally positioned to exploit the advances in online communications and marketing opportunities, and thereby offer an enhanced viewing experience for connected viewers. This connectivity included access to additional textual material available via mobile telephone networks, viral ads and online roleplay games, as well as official and other media marketing and critical coverage in the traditional media outlets and across websites.

Afterword: The Lamp Post

The *Lost* text is complex, non-linear and multilayered: its narrative flow being broken up via the use of flashbacks, flashforwards and flash-sideways; themes and motifs being brought to the fore through the use of repetitions and cyclical mirroring of plot events, or with single events being retold several times from different character points of view; and in the use of parallel time when characters experience temporal displacements, dreams and other forms of foreknowledge. In this way the series constructs and maintains multiple time periods and timelines, and events that are depicted in one episode may be explained or added to only in later episodes, sometimes seasons apart. Combined with semio-narratological codes such as the discourses on science and technology, surveillance and society, this complex narrative form works to produce meaning related to the anxieties of the age, not only in terms of media and technology in their own right, but in relation to socio-cultural themes and the experiences of everyday life.

At the time of writing, it is now ten years since the final episode of *Lost* was transmitted. Looking back, it can be seen that the series represents a focal point in television history. *Lost*, along with similar series like *The X-Files* and *Twin Peaks* that combined science fiction with mystery and investigative drama, can also be seen as a significant form of telefantasy. It marked the transition of cult television from niche programming to the prime time mainstream. As a hugely popular series it facilitated a wider acceptance for previously marginalised genres such as science fiction to be regarded as quality television. As a pivotal series in this respect, *Lost* was part of a broadening of the range of science fiction on prime time television, as well as furthering audiences' understanding of the genre.

At its height, *Lost* attracted over 20 million viewers in the US that saw it winning its timeslot in the Nielson ratings. It reached a high of 23.47 million viewers for episode 1 of season two, though its lowest ratings during seasons 5 and 6 saw a fall to below 10 million. Despite what was often interpreted as declining audience figures as the series progressed, the core fan audience continued to participate in *Lost*'s interactive paratexts and actively engaged in online discussion during later seasons. In a changing viewing landscape, this illustrates the fact that traditionally-measured audience figures no longer necessarily give a true picture of viewership or popularity. *Lost* came at a pivotal moment in the evolution of media consumption patterns that followed. Recording and time-shifting, binge watching of DVD and Blu-ray boxsets, and streaming or online viewing, as well as downloading sites, were all becoming much more commonplace. Although *Lost* was still 'water-cooler' TV discussed the day after transmission, it was also 'must-click' TV, to use Jennifer Gillan's term (2011). In fact, *Lost* became one of the most recorded programmes by viewers, but it also invited interaction with its web- and social media-based material. The fast pace of technological and social media change means that it is now extremely difficult, as Elizabeth Evans concludes, to provide a definitive account of what television means (2011: 179), but *Lost* remains a significant landmark in that changing landscape.

In the context of its paratexts, *Lost* also represents the moment in time when fan culture was being taken on board, and commodified, by the culture industries. Science fiction media has traditionally given rise to merchandise – toys, games, action figures, etc. – and the fan-market for this has long existed, of course. But *Lost* illustrates the way in which the culture industries now use online-based material as a 'mechanism for storyworld expansion' (Harvey, 2015: 30), encouraging audiences to participate in online events associated with the programme. While the various paratexts of *Lost* were not required in order to complete the story given in the TV episodes, they did add depth, fill in details, and offer further interactive experiences. This scenario is now commonplace for series such as *Doctor Who* and *Westworld* (both also series with complex timelines).

One aspect of cult media is longevity, of course, not just in the cultural moment but in continuing to attract attention long after its completion. On the one hand, magazines and online publications published retrospective articles in late 2019 and early 2020 marking the decade since the final season. Writing in *Esquire*, Justin Kirkland reassesses the finale, arguing that it is 'a beautifully simplistic finish to an often convoluted series' (2020). On *Den of Geek*, Alex Bojalad celebrates *Lost* fandom, stating that 'The story of the *Lost* fandom is really the story of how cult fandoms abandoned their cult status and went mainstream with an assist from the burgeoning internet' (2019). This acknowledges the importance of the fan audience in the television/new media landscape. On the other hand, fan activity continues with reviews still being posted on sites such as Amazon and IMDb, new fanworks being uploaded to sites such as the FanFiction archive and An Archive of Our Own, and sellers on Etsy offering *Lost* mugs, posters, badges and clothing – including that for cosplay, embroidery patterns, and even face masks with DHARMA logos. Meanwhile fans and new viewers continue to watch; the series is available on a range of streaming services including Amazon Prime, iTunes, Google Play, IMDbTV and Hulu, making it instantly available for rewatching or finding anew. *Lost* is here and now in the present waiting to be rediscovered.

Writing in *Entertainment Weekly* as *Lost* ended its six-year run, Margaret Lyons claimed that, 'we may never fully uncover all the mysteries of *Lost*'s island' (2010). With its concluding double-length episode 6.17 'The End' coming out of left field and not quite resolving all – or any – of the enigmas set up in the narrative, the pleasures and appeals of *Lost* have since been a continuing subject of debate. In comparing *Lost* with *The Prisoner*, and arguing that both occupy a similar niche in terms of their ambiguous narrative closure, Joanne Morreale (2010: 185) says that: '*Lost* offers hope rather than despair, and that will be its legacy in television history'. Not least it can be considered as one of a small number of television dramas – *The Prisoner*, *Twin Peaks*, *The Sopranos* (1999-2007) and *St Elsewhere* (1982-88) among them – that will remain in the memory as stories that are never quite resolved nor forgotten. Whether viewers find *Lost*, in whole or in part, satisfying, frustrating and disappointing or captivating, intriguing and mind-blowing, the series has assured itself a position not just in television history, but in the emergence of convergence culture and transmedia storytelling.

Notes

1. Viewable at https://www.youtube.com/watch?v=Ug1GAOXpIjU (accessed 8 September 2020).
2. Viewable at https://www.youtube.com/watch?v=3eIPNOMW7F0 (accessed 10 September 2020).
3. Available at https://www.ted.com/talks/j_j_abrams_the_mystery_box (accessed 10 September 2020).
4. Viewable at https://www.youtube.com/watch?v=zvZV0ilxZ0U (accessed 12 October 2020).
5. Viewable at https://www.youtube.com/watch?v=kV38QTyr-kI (accessed 28 September 2020).
6. Viewable at http://www.youtube.com/watch?v=pRw6PY-cCPU (accessed 8 September 2020).
7. See for example http://thelostmap.blogspot.com (accessed 7 October 2020).
8. This is not restricted solely to mothers and daughters, of course. It is also true of Jack with his father Christian, and Locke with Anthony Cooper.
9. For example, in *The Lost Experience* ARG, the captain of the Black Rock slave ship is Magnus Hanso, presumably an ancestor of Alvar Hanso of the Hanso Foundation.
10. Viewable at https://www.youtube.com/watch?v=yY5vV7bp5z8 (accessed 3 October 2020).
11. Another connection can be identified in the Biblical Daniel being an interpreter of dreams and *Lost*'s Daniel interpreting the strange events on the island as they jump through time.
12. Others include Mikhail Bakunin and Edmund Burke. It is also worth noting that the philosopher Locke was patronised by Anthony Ashley Cooper, Earl of Shaftesbury, and *Lost* Locke's father is another Anthony Cooper (though this is only one of his many assumed names and he is a lot less supportive).
13. See http://archive.hi-res.net/thelostexperience/ (accessed 30 September 2020). Video material viewable at https://www.youtube.com/playlist?list=PL41FC3DA0F099E8CA (accessed 3 October 2020).
14. Video material and walkthroughs of the game elements viewable at https://www.youtube.com/playlist?list=PL25438A8890564124 (accessed 3 October 2020).
15. Available at http://lost.cubit.net/pics/2x17/blastDoorMap.jpg (accessed 7 October 2020).

References

Abbott, Stacey (2009). 'How *Lost* Found its Audience: The Making of a Cult Blockbuster', in Roberta Pearson (ed.), *Reading Lost*. London: I.B. Tauris, pp. 9-26.

Askwith, Ivan and Jonathan Grey (2008). 'Transmedia Storytelling and Media Franchises', in Robin Anderson and Jonathan Gray (eds), *Battleground: The Media, Volume 2*. Westport, CT: Greenwood Press, pp. 519-27.

Ausiello, Michael (2010). 'Early *Lost* Ratings: Solid, Not Spectacular', *Entertainment Weekly* (24 May), http://insidetv.ew.com/2010/05/24/early-lost-finale-ratings/ (accessed 14 August 2020).

BBC News (2005). 'Ratings Soar As Viewers Find *Lost*', *BBC News* (11 August), http://news.bbc.co.uk/1/hi/entertainment/tv_and_radio/4141504.stm (accessed 14 August 2020).

BBC News (2006). 'Lost Ratings Fall With Sky Debut', *BBC News* (20 November), http://news.bbc.co.uk/1/hi/entertainment/6165448.stm (accessed 14 August 2020).

Bernstein, David (2007). 'Cast Away', *Chicago Magazine* (August), http://www.chicagomag.com/Chicago-Magazine/August-2007/Cast-Away/ (accessed 14 August 2020).

Bertetti, Paolo (2017). 'Building Science Fiction Worlds', in Marta Boni (ed.), *World Building: Transmedia, Fans, Industries*. Amsterdam: Amsterdam University Press, pp. 47-61.

Bojalad, Alex (2019). '*Lost*: A history of the Fandom', *Den of Geek* (25 September), https://www.denofgeek.com/tv/lost-a-history-of-the-fandom/ (accessed 17 September 2020).

Brown, Simon (2010). 'Cult Channels: Showtime, FX and Cult TV', in Stacey Abbott (ed.), *The Cult TV Book,*. London: I.B. Tauris, pp. 155-66.

Brugger, Peter (2001). 'From Haunted Brain To Haunted Science: A Cognitive Neuroscience View of Paranormal and Pseudoscientific Thought', in James Houran and

Rense Lange (eds), *Hauntings and Poltergeists: Multidisciplinary Perspectives*. North Carolina: McFarland, pp. 195-213.

Card, Orson Scott (2006). 'What is *Lost* Good For?', in Orson Scott Card (ed.), *Getting Lost: Survival, Baggage and Starting Over in J.J. Abrams' Lost*. Dallas, TX: Benbella Books, pp. 1-20.

Clarke, Morris J. (2010). '*Lost* and Mastermind Narration', *Television and New Media*, 11 (2), pp. 123-42.

Craig, Olga (2005). 'The Man Who Discovered *Lost* – And Found Himself Out of a Job', *The Telegraph* (14 August), http://www.telegraph.co.uk/news/worldnews/northamerica/usa/1496199/The-man-who-discovered-Lost-and-found-himself-out-of-a-job.html (accessed 14 August 2020).

Craig, Steve (2002). *Sports and Games of the Ancients*. Santa Barbara, CA: Greenwood Publishing.

Decker, Wolfgang (1992). *Sports and Games of Ancient Egypt*. New Haven, CT: Yale University Press.

Dena, Christy (2008). 'The Future of Digital Media Culture is All In Your Head: An Argument for Integration Cultures', *Leonardo Electronic Almanac*, 16 (2-3), pp. 1-10.

Dolan, Marc (2010). '*Lost*', in David Lavery (ed.), *The Essential Cult TV Reader*. Lexington: University Press of Kentucky, pp. 149-57.

Evans, Elizabeth (2011). *Transmedia Television: Audiences, New Media and Daily Life*. London: Routledge.

Fernandez, Maria Elena (2005). '*Lost* Takes an Odd Path to Diversity', *Los Angeles Times* (13 February), http://articles.latimes.com/2005/feb/13/entertainment/ca-lost13 (accessed 14 August 2020).

Fiske, John (1988). *Television Culture*. London: Routledge.

Fowler, Alastair (1982). *Kinds of Literature: An Introduction to the Theory of Genres and Modes*. Cambridge, MA: Harvard University Press.

Gallardo-C., Ximena and C. Jason Smith (2004). *Alien Woman: The Making of Lt. Ellen*

Ripley. New York: Continuum.

Geraghty, Lincoln (2009). *American Science Fiction Film and Television*. Oxford: Berg.

Gilbert, Matthew (2005). 'The Games People Play With Names', *The Boston Globe* (10 February), http://www.boston.com/ae/tv/articles/2005/02/10/the_games_people_play_with_names (accessed 14 August 2020).

Gillan, Jennifer (2011). *Television and New Media: Must-Click TV*. London: Routledge.

Gray, Jonathan (2009). *Television Entertainment*. Abingdon: Routledge.

Gwenllian-Jones, Sara (2004). 'Virtual Reality and Cult Television', in Sara Gwenllian-Jones and Roberta Pearson (eds), *Cult Television*. Minneapolis: University of Minnesota Press, pp. 83-97.

Hall, Stuart (1997). *Representation: Cultural Representations and Signifying Practices*. Milton Keynes: Open University Press.

Haraway, Donna (1991). *Simians, Cyborgs and Women: The Reinvention of Nature*. Abingdon: Routledge.

Harvey, Colin (2015). *Fantastic Transmedia: Narrative, Play and Memory Across Science Fiction and Fantasy Storyworlds*. Basingstoke: Palgrave Macmillan.

Hills, Matt (2004). *Fan Cultures*. London: Routledge.

Hilmes, Michelle (2011). *Only Connect: A Cultural History of Broadcasting in the United States*. Boston: Wadsworth.

Hoppenstand, Gary and Ray B. Browne (1987). 'The Horror of It All: Stephen King and the Landscape of the American Nightmare', in Gary Hoppenstand and Ray B. Browne (eds), *The Gothic World of Stephen King: Landscape of Nightmares*. Bowling Green, OH: Bowling Green State University Popular Press, pp. 1-19.

Horkins, Tony (2005). 'Survival of the Fittest', *The Guardian* (6 August), http://www.guardian.co.uk/media/2005/aug/06/tvandradio.guide3 (accessed 14 August 2020).

Jenkins, Henry (1992). *Textual Poachers: Television Fans and Participatory Culture*. London: Routledge.

Jenkins, Henry (1995). 'Infinite Diversity in Infinite Combinations: Genre and Authorship in Star Trek', in Henry Jenkins and John Tulloch (eds), *Science Fiction Audiences: Watching Doctor Who and Star Trek*. London: Routledge, pp. 175-95.

Jenkins, Henry (2006). *Cultural Convergence: Where Old and New Media Collide*. New York: NYU Press.

Johnson, Catherine (2005). *Telefantasy*. London: BFI Publishing.

Kaye, Sharon (2010). *The Ultimate Lost and Philosophy: Think Together, Die Alone*. Hoboken, NJ: John Wiley.

King, Stephen. 1981. *Danse Macabre*. London: Futura.

Kirkland, Justin (2020). 'Sorry, Haters: The *Lost* finale was a powerful, misunderstood ending to one of TV's boldest shows', *Esquire* (23 May), https://www.esquire.com/entertainment/tv/a32631252/lost-finale-meaning-explained-10-year-anniversary/ (accessed 21 September 2020).

Kissell, Rick (2004). 'ABC, Eye Have Quite Some Night', *Variety* (23 September), http://www.variety.com/article/VR1117910869 (accessed 14 August 2020).

Lyons, Margaret (2010). 'Lost Map: Explaining the Island. Sort of.', *Entertainment Weekly* (16 June), http://popwatch.ew.com/2010/06/16/lost-map/ (accessed 14 August 2020).

Mangan, Lucy (2005). 'Has *Lost* Lost the Plot?', *The Guardian* (21 September), http://www.guardian.co.uk/theguardian/2005/sep/21/features5 (accessed 14 August 2020).

Mittell, Jason (2015). *Complex TV: The Poetics of Contemporary Television Storytelling*. New York: New York University Press.

Morreale, Joanne (2010). '*Lost, The Prisoner*, and the End of the Story', *Journal of Popular Film and Television*, 38 (4), pp. 176-85.

Ndalianis, Angela (2005). 'Television and the Neo-Baroque', in Michael Hammond and Lucy Mazdon (eds), *The Contemporary Television Series*. Edinburgh: Edinburgh University Press, pp. 83-102.

Nelson, Robin (1997). *TV Drama in Transition: Forms, Values and Cultural Change*. Basingstoke: Macmillan Press.

Nelson, Robin (2010). '*Life On Mars*', in David Lavery (ed.), *The Essential Cult Television Reader*. Lexington: University Press of Kentucky, pp. 142-48.

Oromaner, Marc (2008). *The Myth of Lost: Solving the Mysteries and Understanding the Wisdom*. Bloomington, IN: iUniverse.

Parks, Lisa (1996). 'Special Agent or Monstrosity? Finding the Feminine in *The X-Files*', in David Lavery, Angela Hague and Marla Cartwright (eds), *Deny All Knowledge: Reading The X-Files*. Syracuse: Syracuse University Press, pp. 121-34.

Pearson, Roberta (2007). '*Lost* in Transition: From Post-Network to Post-Television', in Kim Akass and Janet McCabe (eds), *Quality: Contemporary American Television and Beyond*. London: I.B. Tauris, pp. 239-56.

Penley, Constance (1990). 'Time Travel, Primal Scene and the Critical Dystopia', in Annette Kuhn (ed.), *Alien Zone: Cultural Theory and Contemporary Science Fiction Cinema*. London: Verso, pp. 116-26.

Porter, Lynette and David Lavery (2006). *Unlocking the Meaning of Lost: An Unauthorized Guide*. Naperville: Sourcebooks.

Rennett, Michael (2011). 'Narrative Philosophy in the Series: Fate, Determinism, and the Manipulation of Time', in Randy Laist (ed.), *Looking for Lost: Critical Essays on the Enigmatic Series*. Jefferson, NC: MacFarland, pp. 25-42.

Robinson, Juneko J. (2009). 'Immanent Attack: An Existential Take on the *Invasion of the Body Snatchers* Films', in Scott A. Lukas and John Marmysz (eds), *Fear, Cultural Anxiety and Transformation: Horror, Science Fction and Fantasy Films Remade*. Lanham, MD: Lexington Books, pp. 23-44.

Róheim, Géza and Alan Dundes (1992). *Fire in the Dragon and Other Psychoanalytic Essays on Folklore*. Princeton, NJ: Princeton University Press.

Rosen, Christopher (2010). 'Former ABC Exec Lloyd Braun, the Voice of "Previously, on *Lost*," Says, "I Know What the Smoke Monster Was..."', *New York Magazine*

(1 February), http://nymag.com/daily/entertainment/2010/02/lloyd_braun_interview_lost_voi.html (accessed 14 August 2020).

Schneider, Susan (2009). 'Thought Experiments: Science Fiction as a Window into Philosophical Puzzles', in Susan Schneider (ed.), *Science Fiction and Philosophy: From Time Travel to Superintelligence*. Chichester: John Wiley and Sons, pp. 1-14.

Sellers, Patricia (2004). 'ABC's Desperate Measures Pay Off', *Fortune* (15 November), http://money.cnn.com/magazines/fortune/fortune_archive/2004/11/15/8191109/index.htm (accessed 14 August 2020).

Stewart, James B. (2006). *DisneyWar: The Battle for the Magic Kingdom*. London: Simon and Schuster.

Sutton, Paul (2010). '*The Avengers/The New Avengers*', in Stacey Abbott (ed.), *The Cult TV Book*. London: I.B. Tauris, pp. 61-66.

Taylor, John L. (2003). 'Probing the Limits of Reality: The Metaphysics in Science Fiction', *Physics Education*, 38 (1), pp. 20-26.

Team WWK (2008). 'Our Christmas Gifts to Television', *Eonline* (24 December), http://uk.eonline.com/uberblog/watch_with_kristin/b72784_our_christmas_gifts_television.html (accessed 14 August 2020).

Telotte, J.P. (2008). 'The Trajectory of Science Fiction Television', in J.P. Telotte (ed.), *The Essential Science Fiction Television Reader*. Lexington: The University Press of Kentucky, pp. 1-34.

Thompson, Kristin (2003). *Storytelling in Film and Television*. Massachusetts: Harvard University Press.

Thornham, Sue (2007). *Women, Feminism and Media*. Edinburgh: Edinburgh University Press.

Thornton, Sarah (1995). *Club Cultures: Music, Media and Subcultural Capital*. Cambridge: Polity Press.

Tucker, Ken (2004). 'TV Review: Lost', *Entertainment Weekly* (24 September), http://www.ew.com/ew/article/0,,697505,00.html (accessed 14 August 2020).

Tucker, Ken (2010). '10 Shows That Changed TV Since '90', *Entertainment Weekly* (17 September), https://ew.com/gallery/10-shows-changed-tv-90/ (accessed 14 August 2020).

Tulloch, John and Manuel Alvarado (1983). *Doctor Who: The Unfolding Text*. London: Macmillan.

Wilson, Benji (2005). 'A Trailer Ahead of Its Time', *The Guardian* (25 July), p. 3.

Wood Joley (2007). *Living Lost: Why We're All Stuck on the Island*. New Orleans: Garrett County Press.

Worth, Sarah (2004). 'Narrative Understanding and Understanding Narrative', *Contemporary Aesthetics*, 2, https://contempaesthetics.org/newvolume/pages/article.php?articleID=237 (accessed 14 August 2020).

Zipes, Jack David (1994). *Fairy Tale as Myth/Myth as Fairy Tale*. Lexington, KY: University Press of Kentucky.

Constellations

'This stunning, sharp series of books fills a real need for authoritative, compact studies of key science fiction films. ...the volumes in the Constellations series promise to set the standard for SF film studies in the 21st century.' Wheeler Winston Dixon, Ryan Professor of Film Studies, University of Nebraska

Children of Men – Dan Dinello

"...an impressive, intelligent and perceptive analysis of a film increasingly recognised in retrospect as a classic of modern dystopian cinema." Starburst

Close Encounters of the Third Kind – Jon Towlson

"...a thoroughly researched, lucid, and insightful study that succeeds on multiple levels of inquiry." Extrapolation

Ex Machina – Joshua Grimm

Exploring Ex Machina's ideas about consciousness, embodiment, and masculinity, all through the lens of a misogynist mad scientist, Joshua Grimm argues the result is a fascinating and unique film that immediately established Alex Garland as a breakout voice in the landscape of science fiction film.

Robocop – Omar Ahmed

"...this exceptional monograph... is essential reading for sf and film critics as well as fans who are nostalgic for an era that marked the end of sf as a genuine art form." Extrapolation

www.ingramcontent.com/pod-product-compliance
Lightning Source LLC
Chambersburg PA
CBHW071414300426
44114CB00016B/2299